D1108342

OP 10

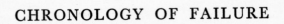

CHRONOLOGY OF FAILURE

THE MACMILLAN COMPANY
NEW YORK · BOSTON · CHICAGO · DALLAS
ATLANTA · SAN FRANCISCO

MACMILLAN AND CO., Limited
LONDON · BOMBAY · CALCUTTA · MADRAS
MELBOURNE

THE MACMILLAN COMPANY
OF CANADA, Limited
TORONTO

CHRONOLOGY OF FAILURE

The Last Days of the French Republic

by

HAMILTON FISH ARMSTRONG

Editor, *Foreign Affairs*
Author, "We or They," etc.

NINETEEN HUNDRED AND FORTY-ONE

NEW YORK · THE MACMILLAN COMPANY

Copyright, 1940, by
THE MACMILLAN COMPANY.

All rights reserved—no part of this book may be reproduced in any form without permission in writing from the publisher, except by a reviewer who wishes to quote brief passages in connection with a review written for inclusion in magazine or newspaper.

Set up and printed. Published October, 1940.

Reprinted January, 1941.
Reprinted April, 1941.

SET UP BY BROWN BROTHERS LINOTYPERS
PRINTED IN THE UNITED STATES OF AMERICA

To

ANDRÉ GÉRAUD

FOREWORD

IN THE FOLLOWING PAGES I have attempted to piece together
a day-by-day account of the "thirty days' war" which followed
the German attack on the Low Countries on May 10, and of
the chief political events during that time and in the ensuing
period of the French collapse. Related events in other countries, including the United States, are also indicated. Gaps
remain in both the military and the political story. We still lack
accurate information about the strength and disposition of the
Allied troops on May 9 and about many of their subsequent
movements, especially in the very first days of the campaign.
Also, despite the "inside stories" being printed in various mag-
azines, there remain important uncertainties about the behavior
of various French political leaders, especially between the
departure of the French Government for Tours on June 10
and the time the armistices with Germany and Italy came
into effect early on June 25.

The account does not pretend to be more than an advance
catalogue of the materials which historians—if there are to be
historians—will later on examine and reëxamine. I simply
attempt to record the main matters that we now know or think
we know; to put them into order; and to emphasize the points
which seem to have been decisive. The story is based partly
on press accounts, partly on my own conversations and obser-

vations during the short time that I was in France just before the fall of Paris, and partly on information supplied from various private sources. I am much indebted to Mr. Charles F. Johnson for assistance in the compilation of material, to Mr. Melville J. Ruggles and Mrs. Marjorie P. Coxe for help in checking it and to Miss Elizabeth King Simeon for preparing the index. The printed sources which have been particularly useful are the "Bulletin of International News," published in London by the Royal Institute of International Affairs, and the *New York Times,* the *New York Herald Tribune,* the *Chicago Daily News,* the *Times* of London and *Le Temps* of Paris.

The chronology is reprinted, with some revisions, from *Foreign Affairs.* The introductory chapter and the two chapters at the end are new. The first describes the situation in the Allied camp on the eve of the great Nazi offensive of May 10. In the others I try to discover the reasons for the French catastrophe and point out some lessons which may be of use to us in the United States today.

H. F. A.

CONTENTS

CHRONOLOGY OF FAILURE

CHAPTER I

THE SETTING FOR THE GERMAN ATTACK

ON MAY 10 Hitler sent his troops into Holland, Belgium and Luxembourg. He chose the moment well. For although there had been repeated warnings of just such a German invasion, the British and French Governments were neither of them in a condition to react to the actual event in instant unison and with a maximum of effectiveness.

The winter had offered both countries an opportunity to improve their preparations against a Nazi attack in the west. It gave them a chance to expand industrial plants, let contracts in America, train pilots, improve fortifications. It provided a chance for repairing political fences in the Balkans and, especially, in Turkey. It provided a chance for putting Mussolini on the spot by offering him the bald alternative of war on the Allied side or war on the side of Germany, a choice which in the first phase of the conflict he could have answered in only one way. It provided a chance for coming to an explicit understanding with Queen Wilhelmina and King Leopold about the military steps to be taken in the event of a Nazi attack on their two countries.

Some of these jobs were well done, or at any rate well started. Some were bungled, and some neglected entirely.

I

In a general way it was perhaps inevitable that the winter should be a period of let-down in the Allied camp. The Nazi colossus had overwhelmed Poland, but then it had paused. Was it really as invincible as its engineers pretended? Or was its mechanized might subject to apparently trifling but perhaps vital defects? Lack of high octane gasoline for airplanes? Or lack of the necessary real rubber for tires? Or lack of molybdenum or some other recondite metal necessary in making armor plate for tanks? Everyone began to hope so. People said to each other that this was not a war like that of 1914–18. It was not a war of men, or even of opposing engines of destruction, but of national reserves, of empires, of colored areas on maps.

Cries of alarm were heard from the Low Countries from time to time. But afterwards word would spread in London and Paris that some unusual concentration of German troops had been ended, or that the fifth columnists suspected of being about to stage a *putsch* had been arrested. In any case, King Leopold and Queen Wilhelmina clung to the thesis that they must act as though they were equally menaced by both Germany and the Allies, though, of course, they knew in their hearts that this was simply not so. Paris and London did not insist on a showdown by informing the two rulers that unless staff plans for joint military action in an emergency had been perfected before that emergency arose, the British and French Armies would not come to their aid but would wait the German shock on the Franco-Belgian frontier. It was easier not to adopt such a strong attitude, just as it had been easier not to take a strong attitude toward Mussolini, but rather to try to bribe him into benevolent neutrality. So it happened that all through the winter the question of just what should be done if Hitler drove into the Low Countries remained without a final decision. And so it happened that all winter the Allies sold Mussolini the gasoline which fuelled his transports to Libya and later on was to fuel his bombers over Tours, Bordeaux, Malta and Suez.

Through the autumn and winter, too, there were long debates, in which political, military and naval leaders of France and Britain joined, as to whether or not Anglo-French armed strength should be exerted away from the western front. The issue was first discussed in connection with the Balkans and the Caucasus. Later it came to a head in connection with projects for giving support first to the Finns, then to the Norwegians. These debates deepened political cleavages both in England and in France and drew lines inside both governments. They also gave an impression of indecisiveness which had a serious effect on the smaller countries of Europe and on Turkey.

Perhaps because various concrete problems like those mentioned above could not be satisfactorily solved, British and French official circles tried to give the impression that they were not very important. This added to the general sense that the winter was "time out" rather than a God-given respite in which the Allies must exert every possible effort to cut down the disparity between their striking power and Hitler's. They tended to rely more and more on the adequacy of defensive tactics to hold him at bay and on the efficacy of the blockade to bring him at last to his knees. This expectation became the general excuse for everything which was left undone or which was only half-done. To the extent that anything was left undone or only half-done the winter worked in Hitler's favor; for in Nazi Germany nothing was left undone or half-done.

On April 9 Hitler broke the apparent truce; he occupied Denmark and invaded Norway. During the following month his troops did not secure complete success. The British expeditionary force hung on in Narvik. But the larger bodies of British troops which had landed at several points on the Norwegian coast, and the French and Polish troops which had accompanied or followed them, were forced to retire. By the first week in May the British people, press and Parliament were busy debating the responsibilities for what seemed more and more clearly to have been a great Allied failure.

On May 9 I was on a steamer bound for Europe. I spent the day largely in listening to the broadcasts from London. Britain was at war with the most formidable military power the world had ever seen. But on this spring day broadcasters from the British capital could spare almost no attention to the actual events of that war because of the necessity for describing the current political crisis in endless detail. The echoes of the great debate over Norway which had rocked the House of Commons the day before, and which had ended by giving the Chamberlain Government a majority of only 81, were still reverberating. Many members of Parliament had abstained from voting; and over 40 members of Mr. Chamberlain's own party had voted against him. Mr. Chamberlain, it was plain, though the B.B.C. skirted around the fact, was clinging desperately to the Prime Ministership. All day he was receiving colleagues and advisers. Some reports indicated that though he insisted on keeping control of the Cabinet he recognized the need for changes in the ranks. What would they be? Mr. Attlee and Mr. Greenwood called at 10 Downing Street in the evening. So did Lord Halifax and Mr. Churchill. It was all very interesting. The radio also brought the information that there was considerable discussion at Westminster as to the proper length of the approaching Whitsun recess.

The Whitsun holiday about which Members of Parliament were concerned that afternoon was never to be enjoyed. And the meeting of the Executive Committee of the Labor Party, called for the day following, May 10, to set the terms for possible Labor participation in the Government, faced, when it actually met, a situation which had been wholly transformed. For about the time that the various gentlemen involved in this busy day of politics were going off to sleep the first *alerte* came from the Luxembourg border.

Copies of the *Times* read at breakfast tables in England on the morning of May 10 were devoted mainly to the goings and comings incident to the Cabinet crisis. They carried no hint, of course, of what had happened across the Channel in the hours between their printing and the time each was delivered, neatly folded, at the subscriber's doorway. There was a dispatch from Amsterdam reporting that the airport there had been closed and that spies (of unnamed nationality) had been rounded up. A five-inch dispatch from Brussels disclosed that there would be a secret session of the Belgian Senate to discuss the activities of "certain foreigners" in Belgium, and that several Germans had been arrested. Two communiqués from Paris told of perfunctory artillery activities and the repulse of some enemy patrols. Yet before Lord Halifax had time to breakfast the Belgian and Dutch Ministers were hurrying to him with the desperate pleas of their sovereigns for help, French airplanes had been destroyed on the ground as far south as Lyon, and the whole German frontier from the Moselle to the North Sea was aflame.

In France there also had been a cabinet crisis over Norway, though it had not come openly to a head. Premier Paul Reynaud had not liked the conduct of French operations in Scandinavia and had decided that General Gamelin, the French Commander-in-Chief, ought to be replaced. This added new intensity to Premier Reynaud's long-standing feud with ex-Premier Daladier, for General Gamelin was known as a Daladier man. It is said that the ex-Premier no longer thought very highly of Gamelin either; but though he had not had the energy himself to replace him, he could not accept the idea that someone else should do it. By May 9 the row had come to such a pitch that when Mr. Reynaud brought the matter up in a Cabinet meeting that afternoon M. Daladier threatened to resign if General Gamelin were replaced; and M. Reynaud was ready to resign if General Gamelin were not replaced. After their sharp discussion, the Cabinet members separated for the night feeling that there would have to be a showdown and probably a new Cabinet the next morning.

But before the new morning dawned Hitler had struck. The French Cabinet closed ranks temporarily, for obviously there could not be a change in the High Command in the very moment of attack. General Gamelin, however, can hardly have felt sure that morning whether or not he was to remain Commander-in-Chief. Perhaps, even, the uncertainty of his position was one of the factors which impelled him to make rather rash decisions about how many troops should be sent into Belgium and Holland and about how far they should be ordered to try to go. This is speculation. But the fact of a definite split in the French Cabinet over the efficiency of the French High Command at the very moment when the campaign opened in the Low Countries is not in doubt.

The Cabinet crisis in Paris merged with the Cabinet crisis in London to provide the Germans, not with the opportunity for a tactical surprise, for that was hardly conceivable, but with an opportunity to act when the men in charge of the destinies of both the Allied Powers were preoccupied with personal and political quarrels.

Chapter II

THE INVASION OF THE LOW COUNTRIES

May 10

Suddenly, without warning or ultimatum, the armed forces of Germany attack the Netherlands, Belgium and Luxembourg. Shortly before dawn Nazi planes bomb the principal Dutch and Belgian aerodromes, and Nazi parachutists make surprise landings at strategic points. Aerodromes through France are also seriously damaged and many French planes are destroyed on the ground. Soon after the commencement of the air raids, German troops cross the Dutch, Belgian and Luxembourg frontiers.

Government communiqués issued later in the day in Berlin, The Hague and Brussels put the start of hostilities at slightly different hours. The resulting confusion is due in part to the difference between Western and Central European time, and to the special Amsterdam time observed in Holland. It seems that the attacks actually begin in force at about 4:30 A.M. Western European time (5:30 A.M. in Berlin; 4:50 in The Hague). By sunrise the Nazi bombers have wrought great and widespread destruction and German troops are pouring across the frontiers into Holland, Belgium and Luxembourg from the Moselle to the sea.

8

The Netherland Government orders its army to resist and appeals for help to London and Paris. Some time after the start of actual hostilities, the German Minister at The Hague delivers an ultimatum. Announcing that "an immense German force has been put into action," he explains that resistance would be "senseless." He claims that his Government possesses "undeniable proofs of an immediately imminent invasion by France and Britain" of the Low Countries, and that the Dutch and Belgian Governments had foreknowledge of the preparations. If the Netherlands decides not to resist, Germany will guarantee its European and overseas possessions. Foreign Minister van Kleffens rejects these allegations and demands; and he states that because of the attack the Netherlands now finds itself at war with the Reich. Queen Wilhelmina later issues a proclamation emphasizing that her Government has followed a course of "strict neutrality during all these months," and making "a flaming protest against this unprecedented violation of good faith and violation of all that is decent between cultured States."

Meanwhile, the Belgian Cabinet has been in emergency session since 1 A.M., after receiving news of heavy German troop movements at 9:30 the previous evening. King Leopold takes command of the forces in the field. General mobilization is ordered. Great Britain and France are requested to implement their guarantees. Early in the morning, but after Brussels, Antwerp, and other cities have already been bombed and when severe fighting is already in progress, the German Ambassador to Belgium calls on Foreign Minister Spaak.

M. Spaak informs him that Germany once again has committed an unwarranted act of aggression against Belgium, and
that Belgium will resist with all her strength.

At 7 A.M. Dr. Goebbels broadcasts to the German people.
As in the case of the invasion of Norway, the German explana-
tion is that an attack had to be made in order to forestall an
attack which was being planned by the Allies. He cites the
anti-German attitude of the Belgian and Dutch press, as also
the extensive military preparations of the Belgian and Dutch
Governments. At 8:25 A.M. Foreign Minister von Ribbentrop issues a memorandum to the German and foreign press
along similar lines. Leaving for the Western Front, Chancellor Hitler issues a proclamation to his troops stating that the
hour has come for the great battle which "will decide the
destiny of the German people for the next thousand
years."

Some hours after the first German air attacks, Allied troops
cross into Flanders and Luxembourg. (In the evening, Premier Paul Reynaud of France in a short radio address announces that the Allied troops began moving between 7 and
8 A.M.) Later information will indicate, however, that
although German attacks have long been predicted, they
nevertheless profit at the outset from eleventh-hour indecision
on the part of the Allied High Command as to where they are
to be met. There also proves to be some delay in starting
French operations in certain critical regions. This is especially
the case where the French Ninth Army, occupying the right
of the line of French defenses along the Franco-Belgian

frontier, fails promptly to take up and consolidate the
advance defensive positions assigned to it on the Belgian
Meuse.

General Gamelin, Allied Commander-in-Chief, in an Order
of the Day says: "The attack that we had foreseen since
October was launched this morning. Germany is engaged
in a fight with us to the death. The order of the day for
France and all her Allies are the words: Courage, energy,
confidence." Officials at the French War Ministry mention
Lyon, Nancy, Calais, Laon, Lille, Colmar, Luxeuil, Béthune,
Abbeville and Lens among the places bombed. Forty-four
enemy planes are brought down on French territory. French
plane losses are not mentioned. The German attacking force
is put by the Ministry at 29 divisions.

Meanwhile, the Dutch are falling back to the line of the
Maas (Meuse) River and the upper Ijssel, where they prepare to offer stubborn resistance, blowing up bridges and
opening the dikes which are part of the Netherland defense
system. But already in the first hours—minutes, almost—the
Germans have gained important strategical advantages. So
quick is their advance that the Dutch fail to blow up certain
vital bridges on the Maas, notably at Maastricht in the "penin-
sula" of Dutch territory reaching down between Germany and
Belgium towards Liège. The Belgians are thereby put at a
serious disadvantage, since Maastricht commands the eastern
end of the Albert Canal. But the Belgian defenses are being
penetrated further north also. German troops appear on the
Meuse north of Liège, near where Uhlans made an early cross-

ing in 1914. German bombing planes continuously attack all the Belgian positions in this area. *Before the morning is over the Germans have already effected crossings of the Meuse near Maastricht and of the Albert Canal between Maastricht and Hasselt.* Belgian defenses on the Canal were expected to hold at a minimum for five days. The Germans have taken them in as many hours. According to the Belgian version, the officer charged with blowing up two vital bridges near Maastricht is killed by a bomb at the moment he is preparing to fulfill this duty. (This is announced by the Belgian Premier, M. Pierlot, over the radio on May 12. His statement, however, does not admit that these developments occurred until May 11.) Also of great importance is the fact that one of the Liège forts, said to be Eben Emael, is (according to tomorrow's German communiqué) "put out of action." Luxembourg is entirely defenseless and during the day is completely overrun. The Grand Duchess Charlotte and her family flee to France.

An attempt is made to adjust internal French political differences by giving Louis Marin and Jean Ybarnégaray, rightist Deputies, places in the Cabinet as Ministers of State. The personal conflict between Premier Reynaud and Defense Minister Daladier, which has been a matter of comment in Paris for some time, is also smoothed over temporarily. In recent days it had been particularly acute, due to M. Reynaud's desire to replace M. Daladier's man, General Gamelin, as Commander-in-Chief. The dispute is resolved for the moment in General Gamelin's favor, because the start of actual hostilities on a large scale makes a sudden change in the High Command difficult if not impossible.

In London, meanwhile, Foreign Secretary Halifax has received both the Belgian Ambassador and the Dutch Minister before 6:30 A.M. They inform him that their countries have been invaded and are resisting, and transmit appeals for Allied assistance. The British War Cabinet meets at 8 A.M., and again at 11:30. At the latter meeting the service chiefs report that arrangements to assist the two invaded countries are, in the words of the *Times* diplomatic correspondent, "in train." At noon the Dutch Foreign Minister, Mr. van Kleffens, and the Colonial Minister, Mr. Welter, arrive in England by air and are received at the Foreign Office in the afternoon. Later the full Cabinet meets. *Shortly before 6 P.M., Prime Minister Chamberlain has an audience with the King and tenders his resignation. Five minutes after he leaves, the King receives Winston Churchill and asks him to form a Cabinet to include the Opposition.* Mr. Chamberlain broadcasts at 9 P.M. explaining the reasons for his resignation.

News of the German invasion is flashed to the Netherland East Indies, where the Dutch authorities seize 19 German ships and intern their crews, as also all Germans of military age.

In Washington, President Roosevelt promptly instructs Secretary of the Treasury Morgenthau to "freeze" all moneys and credits of Belgium, the Netherlands and Luxembourg. Later in the day, addressing the Pan-American Scientific Congress, the President declares that the American people "are

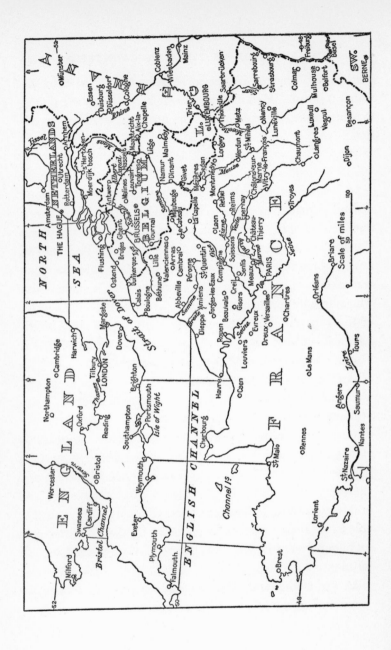

shocked and angered by the tragic news" from the three invaded countries. He adds that it would be a "mistaken idea"
to believe that geography makes the Americas safe from aggression.

MAY 11

In Belgium, the Germans have consolidated their capture
of Eben Emael, key fort in the Liège defenses, strengthening
their control of the junction of the Meuse River and the Albert
Canal. The German communiqué announcing the final surrender of the fort this afternoon says "a new type of weapon"
was used by the attackers. This seems to refer to parachutists
who allegedly descended into the fort and dynamited some
of the gun turrets. (Premier Reynaud's speech on May 21,
q.v., will confirm the use of parachutists at Eben Emael.)
Tanks are pouring into the Belgian defense lines over the
Maastricht bridges. Long lines of refugees are streaming westward out of the battle zone. In southern Belgium, German
armored and motorized columns are making rapid progress
through the difficult terrain of the Ardennes in the direction
of Montmédy and Sedan, meeting with unexpectedly slight
Belgian resistance. The Belgian troops in their flight here and
elsewhere in southern Belgium fail to dynamite roads and
bridges according to plan. German wheeled transport is thus
able to use these roads for the immense movement of men and
supplies required for the advance into France during the next
fortnight.

In the Netherlands, the German troops have crossed the

Ijssel River, where the Dutch had created advance fortifications and where their army had taken a strong stand. Amsterdam and Rotterdam are bombed repeatedly and many fires set. Later estimates will put at 40,000 the number of casualties in Rotterdam alone during the period of resistance. Since the start of hostilities several thousand parachutists have landed in the Netherlands. They are reinforced by resident fifth columnists; by a considerable number of "air infantry," transported by plane and landed at the captured air fields; and by several groups of soldiers brought down the Rhine in "Trojan barges," in the same fashion that German soldiers had been sent to Norway in preparation for the attack on that country. An attempt to seize The Hague by these methods fails. Another, directed at the Waalhaven airport in the suburbs of Rotterdam and the vital north-south bridges in the Moerdijk region, succeeds in maintaining its lodgement. There is little effective defense by Dutch air forces. British combat planes are active in Holland; British bombers attack German troop concentrations in the Rhineland and the Krupp arms works at Essen.

Winston Churchill names a cabinet of national unity. Anthony Eden becomes Secretary for War; Sir Archibald Sinclair, Secretary for Air; and A. V. Alexander, First Lord of the Admiralty. An inner "War Cabinet" of five is composed of Mr. Churchill himself as Prime Minister and Defense Minister; Clement R. Attlee, Lord Privy Seal, and Arthur Greenwood, Minister without Portfolio, representing Labor; Viscount Halifax, who remains as Foreign Secretary; and Neville Chamberlain, who becomes Lord President of the Council.

London announces that, in agreement with the Netherland Government, British and French forces have landed at Curaçao and Aruba, two Dutch possessions off the coast of Venezuela, to prevent possible sabotage of the oil refineries by German residents. In Washington the State Department intimates that it does not look upon this as an infringement of the Monroe Doctrine.

President Roosevelt extends the American neutrality legislation to cover Belgium, the Netherlands and Luxembourg. In reply to an appeal from King Leopold for at least moral support, the President cables him that "the cruel invasion by force of arms of the independent nations of Belgium, Netherlands and Luxembourg has shocked and angered the people of the United States and, I feel sure, their neighbors in the Western Hemisphere." He expresses the hope that the "policies which seek to dominate peaceful and independent peoples through force and military aggression may be arrested, and that the Government and people of Belgium may preserve their integrity and their freedom."

MAY 12

The Germans occupy the northernmost Dutch provinces of Groningen and Friesland, where there were only light defending forces, and reach Harlingen, near the entrance to the Zuider Zee. The Dutch High Command admits that further south the enemy have crossed the Maas and Ijssel Rivers "at various points." An important bridge across the Ijssel east of Arnhem was not blown up in time—"another example," the

London *Times* correspondent fears, "of treachery." By this route German columns have reached the Grebbe "water line" between Amersfoort and the Rhine. The Nazi attack on the Netherland "home front" is being augmented. Additional parachute troops and air infantry land. More important are the activities of resident fifth columnists. These have sabotaged the water defenses at many points. They also put out of commission Amsterdam's water supply, its gas and electricity plants, and its air-raid siren system. Desperate fighting with the parachutists and fifth columnists is still going on in the streets of Rotterdam. The Dutch have not succeeded in recapturing the Rotterdam airport.

In eastern Belgium, a German communiqué at last reveals formally that the Albert Canal has been forced between Hasselt and Maastricht. The Liège forts other than Eben Emael still hold out. Premier Pierlot in the course of a radio address says that their slopes are covered with German corpses. The advance of the Germans near Hasselt brings them within 50 miles of Brussels. Motorcycle units are probably even closer. All day German planes bomb Belgian positions and roads in the rear. Namur and Louvain are also heavily bombed.

Even more important than the German progress south of the Albert Canal is the German operation which has been unfolding in the Ardennes and which now suddenly results in the rupture of the French front on the Meuse. The German communiqués continue to provide very little information about it. *We shall learn subsequently that today the Germans succeed in effecting two crossings of the Meuse, one at Sedan, a French* *town with three bridges, the other lower down the river in* *the region of Dinant.* This part of the front had been entrusted to the French Ninth Army under General Corap (said afterwards to be largely composed of reserve divisions not in good training and with poor morale). The failure of the Ninth Army to prevent the German crossing (not yet disclosed in any communiqué) opens the way for what in the next few days will prove a decisive strategic operation of the German High Command. While the main body of Allied mechanized forces is engaged back of Liège, the French Ninth Army will be broken here on the Meuse.

Not much is revealed about the British and French advance into northern and eastern Belgium. But though details are withheld, the London *Times* correspondent who is with the advancing British troops says they are "already in the heart of the country" and "going forward on oiled wheels." In French military circles it is claimed that so far only advance guards, not main bodies of troops, have been involved in combat. The truth (not yet disclosed) is that General Henri Giraud at the head of the French Seventh Army has already penetrated as far as the Dutch-Belgian frontier near the coast and tomorrow actually will enter Zeeland, the southwestern province of the Netherlands. Some motorized French units in these days even go so far (according to Premier Reynaud's statement of May 21, *q.v.*) as Hertogenbosch, a small place near the junction of the Maas and the Rhine. And in eastern Belgium (the press will learn tomorrow) French tanks are clashing today with German tanks and planes at Tongres and St. Trond, just to the rear of the broken Belgian positions along the Albert Canal near Hasselt and Maastricht. British planes are coöperating by bombing German reserves *en route* from concentration points to the Netherland and Belgian fronts. And a "token force" of about a thousand British troops lands from transports today at the Dutch port of Flushing, in Zeeland.

A retrospective view will show that as of this date British and French aid in the form of motorized divisions has been sent promptly to the Belgians on their first line of defense, the Albert Canal, while in Holland some of General Giraud's advance units have even reached the lower Maas. But it is too late. The Belgian first line has been pierced in the opening hours of the German attack on May 10; and the Germans will never allow the Belgian command a respite in which to re-form its broken troops on the second Belgian line, Namur-Louvain-Antwerp. In moving up towards that line the larger British forces are being impeded by civilian refugees and dispersed Belgian troops; they will reach the River Dyle south of Louvain, but they will be given insufficient time in which to take up positions there properly. For the German forces now beginning to cross the Meuse at Dinant and Sedan, where the French occupation of advance positions has been dilatory and ineffective, will threaten the British-French flank, force General Giraud's rapid withdrawal in the north, and in the end render resistance on the Namur-Louvain-Antwerp line impossible.

Premier Mussolini orders that Italy's western Alpine defenses be further perfected. The move is regarded as political as well as military, for it will both intensify anti-Allied feeling in Italy and worry the Allies. Four new classes—1,000,000 men—are called to the colors. At Rome and throughout Italy demonstrations are arranged by the Fascist Party to arouse a war spirit and to create hostility towards the British. Insulting placards are posted in the streets and Englishmen and other foreigners are involved in many brawls. Italians found buying or reading the Vatican organ, the *Osservatore Romano,* are beaten or thrown into fountains, for it prints the news from both camps at equal length.

The Spanish Foreign Ministry reaffirms Spain's neutrality.

At Tokyo objections are voiced to the landing of Allied forces in the Netherland possessions in the Caribbean. Japan fears that this will be a precedent for disturbing the *status quo* in the Netherland East Indies.

MAY 13

The Nazi Blitzkrieg continues in full violence. The Dutch resist stubbornly but are driven back with heavy losses. Their country is split in two. In the southern sector, German columns link up with the German troops which have taken the Moerdijk Bridge from the air. This bridge across the Maas estuary just south of Rotterdam is of great strategic importance and is the chief Dutch link with Belgium. At this point the Germans are only 30 miles from The Hague. Queen Wilhelmina arrives in England in the evening aboard a British warship. She had been preceded earlier in the day by Crown Princess Juliana and her family.

In Belgium, the Germans drive ahead into the northern plain, northwest of Liège. Here, as in other areas, the German tank columns are supported by low-flying planes. These help disorganize Allied transport not only by direct attacks on it but by bombing and machine-gunning retreating Belgian troops and the refugees from Liège, Namur and other towns who choke the roads in the rear. The Germans say they have now taken Liège itself, but its forts, apart from Eben Emael, still hold. French tanks, the French High Command claims, are counter-attacking in the region of St. Trond, a few miles southwest of Hasselt. Apprehensions rise in French military circles regarding both the conduct of the Belgian Army and the personal rôle of King Leopold. M. Daladier visits Belgian headquarters. It is believed that he remonstrates with the King for not consenting to subordinate his command more thoroughly to the Allied Supreme Command.

The communiqués from both sides provide very little current information about the action on the Meuse between Dinant and Sedan. German tanks and airplanes are hurrying down from northern Belgium to coöperate with the German forces that have come through the Ardennes in the exploitation of a shining German opportunity.

Winston Churchill, appearing in Parliament for the first time as Prime Minister, receives a vote of confidence 381 to 0. He tells the House that he has "nothing to offer but blood, toil, tears and sweat." His only policy, he says, is "to wage war, by sea, land and air," and his only aim is victory—"victory at all costs, victory in spite of all terror . . . for without victory, there is no survival." No survival, he explains, either for the British Empire or for what it has stood for, "no survival for the urge and impulse of the ages, that mankind will move forward towards its goal."

Chapter III

THE COLLAPSE OF HOLLAND AND BELGIUM

May 14

In NORTHERN and eastern Belgium units of the British and French forces which went to the assistance of Belgium and Holland are by now beginning to retire. (M. Reynaud will state on May 21 that the Allied forces in Belgium were not formally ordered to retire until the evening of May 15.) In the south, a series of fierce stabs, executed largely by tanks and motorcyclists, has carried the Germans to the right bank of the Meuse north as well as south of Namur. From Namur to Dinant the French lines hold. British bombers go into action in the effort to eliminate vital bridges which the French have failed to destroy, as well as pontoon bridges which German engineers have been throwing across the river. But south of Dinant the Germans have been concentrating ever stronger forces at the crossing points secured yesterday and the day before. The sector of the line between Dinant and Sedan is becoming the main German front of attack.

The Netherland Prime Minister and other Ministers reach London this morning, and soon after their arrival Queen Wilhelmina issues a proclamation. She declares London the seat of the Netherland Government, but asserts the intention to reëstablish the régime in the home country as soon as possible. She delegates authority there to the military command. The Government has taken these steps, says the Queen, because it wanted to avoid ever being placed in such a position that it would have to capitulate. Consequently, any territories remaining in its hands, including those in the East and West Indies, still form a sovereign state and will be in a position to continue coöperation with Holland's allies.

About noon German bombers begin a terrific attack on Rotterdam which lasts an hour and a half. The anti-aircraft defenses of the city were never perfected. Many incendiary bombs are dropped. Block after block is demolished. The waterfront is set aflame. The Dutch air force has become virtually non-existent. Following the bombing raid, German air troops and squads of fifth columnists which had been expelled or held at bay take the center of the city.

After five days of war, the Commander-in-Chief of the Netherland Army, General Henri G. Winkelman, issues an order late in the afternoon that fighting is to cease. He however excludes Zeeland, the southwestern province which has been cut off by the Germans, and where there is the small body of British troops that landed May 12. It is also explained that the order does not affect the Dutch Navy, which will continue to defend the Dutch colonies in both hemispheres. General Winkelman specifically orders resistance to cease in Rotterdam and Utrecht, "to save the civil population and to prevent further sacrifice of life," and asks that order be maintained "until the arrival of the German regular armies." He concludes his order, which is published by radio at 8 P.M., by saying: "By a vast superiority of the most modern arms the enemy has been able to break our resistance. We have nothing with which to reproach ourselves. We appeal to the Dutch people to remain calm. Ultimately the Netherlands will rise again as a free nation. Long live our Queen!" In a broadcast at 11 P.M. the Commander-in-Chief explains further that "the war was completely one-sided" and that "it was impossible to go on." Losses in the Dutch regular army are stated to have been very heavy, due to its stubborn resistance.

Robert Ley, head of the German Labor Front, writes in today's *Angriff* that National Socialism is now to be considered an article of export. Adolf Hitler's "God-given natural mission," he says, is to make the world happy and reasonable. "He brought Germany to reason," writes Herr Ley, "and thereby made us happy. We are convinced he will bring Europe and the world to reason and thereby make Europe and the world happy. That is his irrevocable mission."

The British Admiralty broadcasts an order that owners of small craft, 30 to 100 feet long, must send in particulars regarding them within 14 days. These vessels become the so-called "Small Vessels Pool," which will prove so valuable during the evacuation from Dunkerque (*cf.* May 26 and May 28–June 4).

The German military successes are having their effect in Italy. Stimulated by the Fascist Party, war fever rises. Anti-British demonstrations throughout the country are climaxed by the burning in Rome, before the British Embassy, of a mock coffin covered by French and British flags and surmounted by an umbrella. Premier Mussolini, smiling, makes three balcony appearances before demonstrators in the Piazza Venezia. The American Ambassador in Rome, Mr. Phillips, decides to advise Americans in Italy to quit the country, and asks American newspapermen in Rome to meet him tomorrow in order that he may inform them of his decision.

MAY 15

The Battle of the Meuse increases in intensity. The French Ninth Army has failed in its efforts to recover the lost bridge-heads, and it has now been completely defeated and overrun. The Germans press westward with all their mechanized and aërial might. In the region of Mézières they do not attack in strength. But the units crossing the river between Namur and Dinant strike forward toward the Sambre, while the forces which have crossed near Sedan press southwest in the direction of Rethel. The French positions at Mézières thus become untenable. In a communiqué today the French admit for the first time that the enemy have crossed the Meuse; it is stated that counterattacks are being made. But the German advance is too swift to permit the bringing up of reinforcements. And the pocket now being formed west and south of the Meuse will be expanded during the coming week until eventually it reaches the Channel and cuts off the British and French forces which on May 10 and 11 were rushed across Flanders from northern France and which are now in retreat. General Corap is dismissed from command of the Ninth Army; General Giraud is appointed in his place.

Further north, the German pressure towards Brussels continues. Louvain, 15 miles east of the capital, is heavily bombarded, but the British Command announces that in this sector the enemy are being held up successfully. German General Headquarters charges that Brussels is the scene of so many troop movements that it no longer can be regarded as an "open city," and threatens it with all the horrors of war if the Belgians do not cease fortifying it and using it for the transit of troops. The situation in the capital is critical. The staffs of many government offices are evacuated to the coast. The telegraph office ceases to function, and a bomb explosion puts the radio out of commission for a period in the evening. The British Air Force makes its heaviest attack so far on German road and rail communications east of the Rhine.

The capitulation of the Netherland Army is signed at 11 A.M. by the German and Dutch Commanders-in-Chief. German mechanized forces occupy The Hague. At Amsterdam the Mayor broadcasts an appeal to the population to show a calm and orderly attitude towards the German troops, who enter the city during the day. Berlin hails the collapse of Dutch resistance as providing airplane bases nearer the heart of England. In Paris, the Netherland Foreign Minister, E. N. van Kleffens, declares in an interview with the foreign press that "the Dutch people have not surrendered" and that "the struggle for a common cause will continue and be kept on to victory." He adds that his country's great possessions, including the Netherland East Indies, exist untouched. "They have been placed at the disposition of the Allies," he says, "and their contributions may be important for the final issue." He estimates that one-fourth of the Netherlands home army of 400,000 have been killed in the five days of the German Blitzkrieg and that 80 percent of the Royal Guard have become casualties.

In the German regions facing Switzerland reports of a concentration of artillery and motorized divisions give the impression that preparations are being made for a German push into Switzerland east of Basel. The Swiss Army completes mobilization.

After a long conference last night with Secretary Hull and other advisers, President Roosevelt drafted a personal appeal to Premier Mussolini not to enlarge the area of the European war. His message (the text of which is not published) is delivered by Ambassador Phillips to Count Ciano in Rome at 10 o'clock this morning. It is eloquent, in some places almost monitory. It warns that if the conflict should spread to include the 200,000,000 people in the Mediterranean area and the Near East there would be much less hope that it could be kept from spreading in the end to include the whole world, with unpredictable results alike for all peoples and for their rulers.

MAY 16

Until now Belgian and British forces have been able to hold off the heavy German attacks in front of Brussels and Antwerp. Bitter fighting has been taking place at Louvain, where the British drive back the German troops which attacked it yesterday. The Belgian Government nevertheless leaves Brussels for Ostend. In accordance with last night's orders of the High Command, British forces in Flanders are beginning to withdraw west of Brussels—a measure which some military critics will afterwards say was long overdue. In the southern sector, German tanks and motorcyclists are penetrating deeply into the French front, supported by low-flying German planes armed with machine guns and bombs. They advance in two main lines. That moving from Givet-Namur just south of the Sambre encounters heavy resistance from the French First Army, which seems to give a very good account of itself. The other moving southwest from Sedan makes progress without very heavy fighting. There is no French army in reserve in this region.

This is a day of uneasiness in Paris, both among officials and public. Stragglers and remnants of units from General Corap's defeated forces have already begun appearing in the outskirts of the city, bringing stories of German domination in the air and of the deadly coördination of German planes and tanks. But the alarm is even more intense in government circles than among the general public, for early in the morning news has come that a German armored column has penetrated almost to Laon, 60 miles west of Sedan and midway between Reims and St. Quentin. At a special meeting called by M. Reynaud in his office and attended by French military chiefs and the Presidents of the Chamber and Senate, General

Gamelin states that in the light of this information he cannot guarantee that the Germans may not reach Paris this very night. The military governor of Paris adds the request that the Government quit the capital at once in order to facilitate measures for its defense. General Gamelin's admission alarms Premier Reynaud and his colleagues. They are determined to continue resistance, but word spreads in official circles that the capital may have to be abandoned. About 11 A.M. M. Reynaud even orders that the Foreign Ministry archives be burned. About three o'clock, however, a reassuring message comes from General Touchon, a vigorous and plucky commander, that the situation around St. Quentin and Laon is better.

In the afternoon Premier Reynaud makes a brief statement to the Chamber of Deputies on the military situation. He is slightly more optimistic than he could have been in the morning. He says that the Government is perfectly aware of the extent of the danger which threatens. He hints at a change in military leadership when he says: "We may be induced to take measures which would have appeared revolutionary yesterday. Perhaps we shall have to change methods and men." He adds: "For every weakness there will be the penalty of death. We must forge new weapons immediately. We are full of hope and our lives count for nothing. One thing alone counts: preserve France." In a broadcast in the evening, the Premier brands as "untrue" the alarming and "most absurd rumors" which have been circulating all day that the Government is preparing to leave the capital. He declares that "the

Government is in Paris and stays in Paris." He also calls false other rumors that the Germans have reached Reims, about 85 miles northeast of Paris, or even Meaux, on the outskirts of the capital, and that they are using "new, irresistible weapons." He admits that the Germans have succeeded in forming a pocket west of the Meuse, but he declares that the French forces are reducing it.

Shortly after Premier Reynaud's radio speech the French Government issues a decree extending the Army Zone to include Paris. The decree, proclaimed without any official explanations, transfers the control of the capital from civilian to military authority. A close guard is posted over the city gates and many foreigners are rounded up. Those of German origin are interned as a precaution against any fifth column uprising. Eight Communists have been sentenced today to terms of imprisonment up to five years for anti-French propaganda.

Prime Minister Churchill arrives in Paris in the evening and goes into conference with M. Reynaud, M. Daladier and General Gamelin.

The Italian Foreign Office confirms without comment the fact of the receipt of President Roosevelt's personal message to Premier Mussolini. The press continues its attack on the British and French, but there are only minor street demonstrations.

President Roosevelt, addressing a joint session of Congress, grimly warns that the United States must be prepared to defend itself if it is not to suffer the fate of the Low Countries, and requests an additional $1,182,000,000 for defense to give the United States a bigger army, navy and air force.

MAY 17

The Germans press their advance in northern Belgium, occupying Brussels, Louvain and Malines. The front of advance in France is being steadily widened, and now reaches from a point ten miles west of Sedan to Maubeuge, in all between sixty and seventy miles. The advancing columns have penetrated into French territory as far as Le Cateau (45 miles from the frontier) and La Capelle; and a new front has been formed north of Rethel. The Germans declare that beyond these points the Allies are "in full retreat" westward, and they claim the capture of 12,000 French prisoners, including two generals.

In London the War Office confirms this evening that the British Army in Belgium retired during last night to positions west of Brussels, "certain adjustments at the front having become necessary." The communiqué says that this readjustment was executed "without interference" and that there "is no question of any collapse or break-through in this sector," as claimed in German official announcements. The Air Ministry adds that the German advance is not being made without cost. It estimates German plane losses in the last seven days at 1,000. However, it is admitted that large German reserves, estimated at 23,000 planes, may enable the Germans to sustain their present large-scale air effort for some time.

Uncounted hordes of refugees choke all roads in Belgium

and Northern France and the congestion impedes the forward movement of troops and guns to the new fronts.

The French admit that the situation is critical. General Gamelin issues an Order of the Day which recalls Marshal Joffre's famous message to the French Armies before the First Battle of the Marne in 1914: "The fate of our country and that of our Allies and the destiny of the world depend on the battle now being fought. English, Belgian and Polish soldiers and foreign volunteers fight at our side. The British Air Force is engaged up to the hilt, like ours. Every unit that is unable to advance must accept death rather than abandon that part of the national territory entrusted to it. As always in the critical hours of our history the watchword today is 'Conquer or die.' We must conquer." The desperate note in this message to the troops gives many Frenchmen the first intimation of the real gravity of the hour.

May 18

The Germans reach the Aisne River. It becomes apparent that their major objective is not Paris but the Channel coast, in the hope of cutting off the British and Belgian armies as well as the French divisions in Belgium. The French do not claim that the German advance has been halted, but say they have slowed it down. The Germans claim that they are within 60 miles of Paris, but the French say 90 miles. French military circles estimate that the Germans are using 80 divisions, 11 of them motorized. They are said to have thrown in from 2,500 to 3,000 tanks, some of them of 70 tons. To deal with the heaviest tanks the French have found they must use their famous 75s, their supply of anti-tank guns and ammunition being far from sufficient.

In Belgium, the Germans announce the occupation of Antwerp, accomplishing in nine days what took sixty-six days in 1914. The Liège and Namur fortifications are isolated but are not yet captured. King Leopold by radio calls on their garrisons to "resist to the utmost."

The British Air Ministry states that the Royal Air Force is carrying the war into Germany with a series of successful raids on communications centers and fuel depots. Bombers have attacked and fired gasoline storage tanks and have damaged other supplies in Bremen and Hamburg.

As a result of the impression made by the German successes Premier Reynaud is enabled to reorganize his Cabinet. He brings in Marshal Pétain as Vice-Premier. The "conqueror of Verdun," now 84 years of age, has recently been serving as Ambassador to General Franco's Government in Madrid. To consolidate political and military leadership, Premier Reynaud himself takes over the Ministry of Defense. M. Daladier, thus replaced, becomes Foreign Minister. M. Mandel is transferred from the Ministry of Colonies to the Ministry of the Interior, indicating that the domestic situation will be controlled with a stronger hand.

In the evening Premier Reynaud broadcasts to the nation. His tone is firm. He informs it of the Cabinet reorganization and calls the situation "serious but certainly not desperate." He pays special tribute to Marshal Pétain, and says he will remain as Vice Premier "until final victory." He concludes: "It is imperative that the feeling of war prevail in all governmental offices as it does elsewhere. Every Frenchman, whether he is in the army or the interior, should this night make with me a solemn oath to win."

The French Government orders a 12-hour day for all workers in aircraft factories, including Sundays and holidays. All engineers engaged in aeronautical design or connected with the aircraft industry are "militarized."

Premier Mussolini replies perfunctorily to the message from President Roosevelt. The *Popolo d'Italia*, dealing with Italy's attitude toward the war, says: "We consider ourselves in fact as having already intervened." Despite Rome's threatening attitude the French High Command has been moving units from the neighborhood of the Italian frontier to fill out the "armée de complement" which it has been trying hastily to assemble between Laon and Paris.

The 21 republics of the Western Hemisphere make public the text of a joint declaration protesting strongly against the German invasion of the Low Countries. The document asserts that the American republics "consider unjustifiable the ruthless violation by Germany of the neutrality and sovereignty" of the countries attacked.

MAY 19

The German salient or pocket, as it is called in the French press, is being extended by a series of quick German stabs. The front now stretches from the Sambre to the Aisne Rivers, and includes the upper valley of the Oise. There is extreme pressure on the northern side of the pocket between Le Cateau and St. Quentin, which latter city the Germans claim to have captured. This presages a push towards the Channel in collaboration with the German troops gathering to the south of Brussels. In the fighting northeast of St. Quentin the Germans are using masses of tanks. The French deny the loss of St. Quentin and insist that in this region their stubborn resistance is on the whole successful. The German High Command states that since the beginning of the campaign ten days ago they have taken 110,000 prisoners, exclusive of Hollanders, and numerous guns.

The withdrawal of the British and Belgians from Belgium is reported to be proceeding "satisfactorily." Their precarious situation is plain to the High Command but is not discussed in the press and is not yet grasped by the general public. The British troops are taking up positions north of Cambrai, with the Belgians on their left (to the east) and the French First Army on their right. Ostend, where the Belgian Government has its headquarters, is bombed several times.

Berlin reports that the last bit of resistance in the Netherlands proper has been crushed with the surrender of the Island of Walcheren, in Zeeland. The Netherland Legation in Paris states that at least 100,000 people were killed and a third of the city destroyed during the German air attacks on Rotterdam.

In the evening the French Government announces that, after consultation with the British, 73-year-old General Maxime Weygand has been appointed Chief of the French General

Staff and Allied Commander-in-Chief in all theatres of opera-tions, supplanting General Gamelin. Rumors begin to be heard in Paris of the arrest of French officers responsible for the break-through at Sedan and other places, and of the dismissal of various Préfets who have permitted the chaotic civilian exacuation of threatened areas.

Prime Minister Churchill, in a speech broadcast to the world, summons the British people to total war against Germany. It is, he says, "a solemn hour for the life of our country, of our Empire, of our allies, and above all of the cause of freedom." The Germans "have broken through the French defenses north of the Maginot Line and strong columns of their armored vehicles are ravaging the country, which for the first day or two was without defenders." He says, however, that the French armies are being regrouped, and he looks with confidence for the stabilization of the front in France. When that time comes, he warns, the British must expect to have turned upon them "that hideous apparatus of aggression which dashed Holland into ruins and slavery." Calling for the utmost exertions, he hints at drastic sacrifices by capital and labor. "I have received from the Chiefs of the French Republic," he continues, "and in particular from its indomitable Prime Minister, M. Reynaud, the most sacred pledges that, whatever happens, they will fight to the end, be it bitter or be it glorious. Nay, if we fight to the end it can only be glorious."

Count Ciano, the Italian Foreign Minister, speaking at Milan at a celebration honoring the first anniversary of the "pact of steel" with Germany, declares that "Italy cannot remain absent from the present terrible struggle which will forge the destinies of the world." Her aspirations, he says, are well known. The Fascist crowd breaks into frenzied cheering and cries of "Corsica! Nice! Savoy!"

In the United States, Charles A. Lindbergh broadcasts a speech in which he declares that the United States "must stop this hysterical chatter of calamity and invasion that has been running rife the last few days." He declares that the United States cannot be invaded successfully by air. He denies that the country is in any danger unless it meddles in matters which do not concern it. He refrains from comment indicating any preference between the contending European belligerents, and does not reveal that he feels the outcome will necessarily affect American interests.

MAY 20

A Council of Ministers is held in Paris. Marshal Pétain gives a pessimistic report. He refers to indications that strategic cohesion among the various French armies has begun to disappear.

The German High Command announces that its forces have captured Laon, 75 miles northeast of Paris. But the main German drive is seen definitely to be towards the Channel rather than towards Paris, with the next immediate objective Péronne. Indeed (though no hint of this appears in today's press) there is reason to believe that on this date German tanks and motorcycle units have already passed around Péronne and are heading down the valley of the Somme towards Amiens. Reports reach military circles in Paris that advance German motorcycle units have even dashed into the suburbs of Amiens and have been destroyed only after causing great confusion and terror. Amiens is only 70 miles from the capital. The evening is one of alternating alarming and reassuring news.

General Ironside, Chief of the British Imperial Staff, visits B. E. F. headquarters in Flanders for consultations with General Gort and with Generals Billotte and Blanchard, French commanders in the north. A Franco-British counter-offensive is planned for tomorrow. The part of the Royal Air Force which has been made available for service on the Continent is exerting great efforts to disrupt German lines of communication.

Field Marshal Goering, on a brief visit to Berlin, gives a press interview. He likens Chancellor Hitler to Frederick the Great, and says that he is wholly responsible for the German plan of campaign. Hitler works out in advance all phases of the offensive, says Marshal Goering, and even "outlines minor actions."

Hundreds of Belgian trawlers have been arriving at ports on the northern coast of France loaded with refugees. Belgians, and added hordes of refugees from northern France, continue to stream across the country. They move in box cars and by road—in private motors, business vehicles, farm wagons, hand carts, on bicycles and on foot.

CHAPTER IV

THE BATTLE OF FLANDERS

MAY 21

The German spearhead reaches the Channel. Nazi motorized units have taken Péronne and Amiens and followed the Somme down to Abbeville. They do not encounter any strong forces here and continue at full speed toward Boulogne. They also take Arras. The Belgian, British and French troops in western Belgium and northeastern France are thus cut off between the German columns and the Channel. The number is estimated by the German High Command at up to a million men. On the southern side of the great pocket, Rethel falls to the invaders. The furthest point of German penetration in the direction of Paris is not known precisely.

Premier Reynaud makes an important address in the afternoon to the French Senate. He says that "the country is in danger" and that it is his duty to tell the truth about what has happened. He begins by explaining the main elements of the French defense position as it was at the start of this campaign:

"Holland, Belgium and Luxembourg having been invaded, the left wing of the French Army left its fortifications between

Sedan and the sea and pivoting on Sedan went forward to a line between Sedan and Antwerp, and even to Hertogenbosch in Holland. Confronted with this situation, which he had foreseen and provided for, the enemy launched a formidable attack against the hinge of the French Army which was behind the Meuse between Sedan and Namur.

"The Meuse, which is in appearance a difficult river, had been mistakenly considered as a serious obstacle to the enemy. For that reason the French divisions which had been charged with its defense were not numerous and were spread out along a great length of river bank. Moreover the troops of General Corap [the French Ninth Army] which were in position there were less solidly officered and less well trained, the best troops having been sent on the wing which advanced into Belgium. While it is true that the Meuse is a river which appears difficult, it is precisely because it is sinuous, enclosed and wooded that it is difficult to defend. Flanking fire by machine guns is impossible there. On the other hand infiltration by manœuvring troops is easy. To that should be added that over half of the infantry divisions of the Corap Army had not yet reached the Meuse although it had the shortest movement to make, being nearest the pivot.

"That is not all. Through unbelievable faults, which will be punished, bridges over the Meuse were not destroyed. Across these bridges the Panzer divisions passed to the attack, preceded by fighting planes which attacked our scattered, badly organized, badly trained divisions. You understand now the disaster—the total disorganization of the Corap Army.

It was in that way that the hinge of the French Army was forced."

Premier Reynaud continues that when he took over the War Ministry he found that the breach opened in the French defenses as a result of the above developments was already over 60 miles wide. "Through this breach," he says, "a German army composed of armored divisions followed by motorized divisions had poured, and, after opening a large pocket in the direction of Paris, was turning toward the west and the sea, taking in the rear our whole system of fortifications along the Franco-Belgian frontier and threatening the Allied forces still engaged in Belgium, to whom the order to retire had not been given until the evening of May 15." In the last 48 hours, he says, the situation has become worse. The High Command has received information that the Germans have taken Arras and Amiens "and even that a bridgehead has been established at Amiens south of the Somme."

In explaining how this all came to pass, M. Reynaud says that the morale of the French troops is not in question. "The truth is," he said, "that our classic conception of warfare has run counter to a new conception. The basis of this conception is not only in the massive use of armored divisions and of fighting airplanes; it is in the disorganization of the enemy rear by deep raids by parachutists, who in Holland just failed to capture The Hague and who in Belgium seized the most powerful fort of Liège. I shall not speak about false news and telephone orders to the civilian authorities, provoking precipitate evacuations."

The French Premier here recalls the black days of the last war which were lived through successfully. He points out that two of the heroes of those days again are serving their country, Pétain and Weygand. He makes a plea that the whole population rise to the heights of their capabilities in the service of France. He warns that "no weakness will be tolerated," that "death is inadequate punishment for any error against the vital interests of the country," and that "while our soldiers are dying there will be no more dilatory procedure against traitors, defeatists and cowards."

Supplementing the Reynaud speech, authoritative quarters in Paris report that General Corap was absent from the headquarters of the Ninth Army on the night the Nazi attack began. Today Berlin tells of the recent capture, apparently on May 19, of the new commander of that Army, General Henri Giraud. The first story is that he was taken prisoner as he arrived at his new headquarters in a château in the Cambrai sector; it seems afterwards that he was captured in a tank while on a visit to encourage brigade officers in the front lines. The War Ministry in Paris admits tonight that it has been "out of communication" with General Giraud for 48 hours. Last night's alarm in official circles in the capital is renewed. Reports are again heard that the Government is preparing to move.

General Weygand has made a visit today by plane across the enemy lines to the French headquarters north of the Somme. He does not visit British headquarters or see General Gort. But General Billotte later transmits Weygand's plan to General Gort and to King Leopold at Ypres. The plan is for an Anglo-French drive southward from Valenciennes and Douai simultaneously with a French drive northward from below the Somme, the aim being, of course, to close the German gap. Meanwhile the British have begun the counter-attack agreed upon yesterday, and register some progress. But they will later claim (in a semi-official statement, July 7) that the French were unable to move simultaneously, as planned.

MAY 22

Back in Paris from his visit to Flanders, General Weygand reports to Premier Reynaud. M. Reynaud passes on to the public the General's words that he is "full of confidence, if everyone does his duty with driving energy." Some military circles in Paris say that the General did not profess "confidence" so much as "determination." Premier Reynaud adds his own conviction that "if we hold for a month—and we shall hold as long as it is necessary—we shall have covered three-quarters of the road to victory."

During the morning Prime Minister Churchill arrives in Paris and at once confers with Premier Reynaud and General Weygand. He hears General Weygand's report on the military situation and his demands as to the course of action to be taken by the British forces in the north. Immediately afterwards he returns to London.

The Allies recapture Arras, and there is hard fighting south of a line between that city and Cambrai, where the French

Seventh Army is making a desperate effort to extricate itself by cutting its way southward. But there is no serious attempt to cut the German salient by a drive from the south. The main French Army seems not to be in a position for an offensive. It is busy hurrying up troops to positions south of the Somme and the Aisne, which rivers are to be General Weygand's new line of defense.

At the tip of the German spearhead German motorized units are attacking Boulogne. Port installations there and at Ostend, Dunkerque, Calais and Dieppe are being bombed, evidently with the aim of hampering the evacuation of the British troops caught in Flanders. German planes also bomb and set fire to stations in the important railway cities of Compiègne and Creil, the latter only 30 miles from Paris, and bomb Senlis, Chantilly and other nearby towns. British planes in turn bomb bridges across the Meuse, and Ruhr railway centers.

The British Parliament in two hours and a half passes the "Emergency Powers (Defence) Act, 1940," an unprecedented measure giving the Government the right to conscript every person and every piece of property and all the financial resources in the realm. The Government receives full power over industry, property and labor to insure the maximum war effort. The excess profits tax is raised to 100 percent. The British Parliament also passes a bill providing that the death penalty may be imposed in grave cases of espionage and sabotage.

Italy marks the first anniversary of the signing of the alli-

ance with Germany by press articles eulogizing the states-
manship which brought together two nations united in common aims. King Victor Emmanuel III confers the Order of
the Annunziata on Field Marshal Goering, thus making him
a "cousin."

Increasing numbers of refugees are streaming west and
south through France. Their plight awakens American concern and Ambassador Bullitt communicates with President
Roosevelt regarding the possibility of American Red Cross
aid.

MAY 23

The British have held their slight gains north of the German gap, but today their right is menaced by a German
advance from Lens (just north of Arras) and they are forced
to withdraw. General Weygand is in Flanders for the second
time in three days. French Channel ports, especially Boulogne and Havre, are heavily bombed.

In the afternoon, Prime Minister Churchill informs a grave
House of Commons of the German successes. He admits that
the German armored columns which forced their way through
the breach in the French defenses are advancing against the
rear of the British and other Allied troops in Belgium. He
confirms the fact that Abbeville is in German hands, and that
heavy fighting is in progress around and in Boulogne. The
Prime Minister adds that General Weygand is conducting
the operations involving all the Allied Armies "with a view
to restoring and reconstituting their combined front." In the

evening Boulogne is relinquished to the Germans, after desperate resistance by Guards regiments and after demolition of the port installations. Survivors are taken off on British destroyers under heavy fire.

A military spokesman in Paris states that since May 10 at least 1,000 German planes have been brought down on French soil. The French Cabinet decides that no department shall be evacuated without a written order of the High Command, and that none of the administrative services shall leave Paris. It also decides that there shall be no evacuation of industries, except for the continued transfer of munitions factories. Forty Communists are arrested at Avignon.

In London, Sir Oswald Mosley and eight of his Fascist workers are arrested and the headquarters of the British Union of Fascists is raided by the police. Other Right and Left extremists are taken into custody also as the British Government moves to short-circuit fifth column activities. Among them is Captain A. H. M. Ramsay, M. P., who is arrested under the defense laws as they stood before they were recently amended.

MAY 24

The Battle of Flanders still rages. The Germans state they have pushed up the coast as far as Calais. Tournai is captured. There is sharp fighting in the streets of Ghent. The plight of the refugees within the Ghent-Abbeville pocket is a mass tragedy. The last fort at Maubeuge is captured. General Weygand, back from his second visit to the forces in the north, reports to M. Reynaud. The French evening communiqué admits ominously that "the continuity of the front has not been reëstablished"—implying that the reuniting of the British-French-Belgian forces in Flanders with the main body of the French armies is no longer to be expected.

Later accounts by French political spokesmen (*e.g.* Foreign Minister Baudouin's newspaper interview at Bordeaux, July 5) will criticize the extent of the British effort in these days. They will allege that General Ironside has hesitated at a vital moment to order British troops to take necessary risks in striking southward and that this is the reason for the failure of the Allied attempt to close the German corridor to the coast. "If the British Army had obeyed Weygand's orders," M. Baudouin will say, "the gap would have been closed." The British will reply (June 7) that: 1, they agreed to counterattack on May 21, and did, whereas the French did not; 2, they were forced to withdraw on May 23, as the Germans had appeared on their right flank and threatened to encircle them entirely; 3, they nevertheless agreed on May 24 to execute the Weygand plan for a simultaneous attack on the Germans from both north and south, and that Generals Gort and Blanchard (General Billotte had meanwhile died of automobile injuries) fixed on May 26 for it to begin; 4, but the next day, May 25, the Belgians were routed, exposing the British left flank and necessitating a withdrawal of troops to support the Belgian front. A statement of the British semiofficial view will conclude: "The plan drawn up by General Weygand was excellent, but it came too late. The disaster which took place was unaffected by anything that happened between May 23 and 26, and was in no sense the fault of General Weygand. It was due to the faulty dispositions of General Gamelin."

The Germans claim that in Brussels they seized diplomatic documents which will provide a sensation when published. The hint is that they will reveal Belgian and Dutch connivance in Allied war plans.

M. Mandel, French Minister of the Interior, calls on all government officials to work a minimum of 52 hours a week and to keep their offices open 12 hours a day. He dismisses a number of Préfets and other functionaries. He also undertakes new measures against fifth columnists.

King George VI, addressing his 500,000,000 subjects in celebration of Empire Day, warns that Hitler's ultimate aim is "the conquest of the world." "There is a word," he says, "which our enemies use against us—Imperialism. By it they mean the spirit of domination and the lust of conquest. We free peoples of the Empire cast that word back in their teeth. It is they who have these evil aspirations." The peoples of the Empire, he says, "have risen in just wrath against a thing which they detest and despise. Nothing can shake their resolution. In perfect unity of purpose they will defend their lives and all that makes life worth living."

Lord Halifax gives a Spanish correspondent a most cordial interview regarding Anglo-Spanish relations. It is confirmed in London that Sir Samuel Hoare will be appointed Ambassador to Spain on a special mission.

A British Air Ministry communiqué states that more than 1,500 German planes have been destroyed in the two weeks since the war began in the Low Countries.

The 25th anniversary of Italy's entry into the First World War on the side of the Allies is marked by an intensification of anti-Allied propaganda. The Government "postpones" the departure of all trans-Atlantic liners scheduled to sail from Italian ports in the near future.

The British Ambassador to the United States, Lord Lothian, carries to Secretary Hull an appeal from the British, French and Belgian Governments for aid in succoring the huge numbers of refugees who are fleeing before the advancing German armies.

The House of Representatives in Washington passes by 391 votes to 1 a defense bill to allow unlimited expansion of the Army Air Corps, soon after President Roosevelt announces plans for training 50,000 volunteer airplane pilots during the fiscal year starting July 1.

MAY 25

The Battle of Flanders moves into a new phase as the German High Command announces the closing in of its troops around much of the Belgian Army, the remnants of the First and Seventh French Armies, and the bulk of the British Expeditionary Force. Calais, Ostend and Dunkerque remain in Allied hands. Calais is being defended desperately by a small British force. The aim is to compel the Germans to concentrate armored units against this city instead of against

Dunkerque, where the evacuation of the trapped British and French armies is to take place, and also to give the French time to carry out flooding operations at Gravelines, between Calais and Dunkerque. On the eastern side of the German ring the capture is reported of Ghent and Courtrai. The Germans say their next objective will be to cut the trapped forces into small detachments and to dispose of them piecemeal. The Belgian forces are being subjected to a particularly heavy attack. They are thrown into confusion, with most serious military and political results.

The French assert that they are making frequent counter-attacks in the Somme region, but do not claim that they have been able to retake the lost bridgeheads on the south bank. About operations further south the French communiqué is fairly optimistic. It says that "Between the Aisne and the Meuse activity continues as fierce as ever. However, since yesterday we dominate the enemy." Subsequent events will not substantiate the latter claim, though it seems to be true that on this date in this southern part of the active front only small German advances are registered.

The French War Ministry issues a communiqué headed "Penalties," announcing the dismissal from their commands of fifteen French generals, including army and corps commanders, several divisional commanders and other high officers. Their commands have already been taken over by new men appointed by General Weygand. Simultaneously, Minister of the Interior Mandel dismisses eight senior police officials in the Département du Nord.

The most important events of the day concern Belgium, though they are not yet known publicly. Several high Belgian officials, including Premier Pierlot, Minister of Foreign Affairs Spaak, Defense Minister General Denis and Minister of the Interior Vanderpoorten, arrive in London. Subsequent revelations in an interview by M. Spaak on May 29 will indicate that *King Leopold has already reached the decision to surrender the Belgian Army.* The Ministers are come to England to discuss the future course of the Belgian Government. The King's decision was taken this morning at 5 o'clock at Wynondal Castle, south of Bruges, following an all-night argument with Pierlot, Spaak and two other Ministers.

MAY 26

The French only now acknowledge the German occupation of Boulogne. They claim that elsewhere their lines are holding. Paris dispatches speak repeatedly of the heavy price in dead and wounded the Germans are paying to keep their pressure up, but admit that it is not lessening. The British are attempting to maintain their positions and also aid the Belgians. The German High Command reports the capture of Calais (denied by the Allies), new fighting between the Aisne and the Meuse, accentuated pressure on the Somme, and the repulse of enemy attacks on the northern front. London reports a four-hour air battle over the French coast between Dunkerque and Calais, as well as the bombing of German columns near Boulogne and in the River Lys sector.

In London, Premier Pierlot and Foreign Minister Spaak

consult with Foreign Secretary Halifax. Later in the day
Premier Reynaud arrives in London by plane for a brief visit.
He confers with Prime Minister Churchill and other members
of the War Cabinet on the military and strategic situation
confronting the Allies, the problems arising from the increasingly hostile attitude of Italy, and the doubtful attitude of
King Leopold.

While M. Reynaud is still in London it is announced that
Lieutenant General Sir John Greer Dill has been appointed
Chief of the British Imperial Staff, replacing General Sir
Edmund Ironside, who becomes Commander-in-Chief of the
Home Forces.

The British Admiralty this evening makes its first call on
the "Small Vessels Pool" (cf. May 14) to provide boats to
help in withdrawing troops from Dunkerque. These and other
volunteer craft of every conceivable sort and size will act
courageously and adventurously during the coming week in
conjunction with naval vessels under the Dover Commander,
Vice-Admiral Sir Bertram H. Ramsay.

The French Government warns that the Germans are issu-
ing false orders to the French civil authorities, often over the
telephone. Announcement is made of the dismissal of police
chiefs in several cities, including Lille and Valenciennes in the
Flanders battlefield area. An official order is issued calling on
all foreigners over 15 years old who have arrived in France
since May 10 to report to the authorities before May 31.

The signs of approaching intervention by Italy on the side of
Germany become stronger. Premier Mussolini confers with his
high army officers and with munitions manufacturers. The

text is published of a bill to "control citizens in wartime." The
circulation of private vehicles using gasoline is to cease on
June 1 except for those with special permits. Giovanni Ansaldo, in his weekly broadcast to the armed forces, says:
"Hitler has broken the steel ring round Germany. So we,
under the guidance of the Duce, will break the bonds impris-
oning Italians in the Mediterranean." Virginio Gayda boasts
that Italian "non-belligerency" is forcing the Allies to keep
about 1,200,000 men idle on the borders of Italy and her
colonies, as well as in the Near East, and notes that "this is
solid, silent help which Italy has given Germany during these
eight months of war." The word heard on every side in Rome
is that Italy will enter the war between June 10 and 20. By
then, it is said, the Germans will have taken Paris and have
their major offensive against England well under way.

President Roosevelt, in a radio address to the nation on the
state of the national defense, assures the country that whatever
may be needed will be done to secure the armed defenses of
the United States at this time, when the world "is threatened
by forces of destruction." He says the United States will build
its defenses to whatever heights the future may require, and
voices confidence that it will not have to abandon its democratic way of life in the effort to match the strength of the
aggressors.

MAY 27

The area occupied by the Allies in the north is being steadily
constricted. Their armies are forced to abandon the salient
which they have maintained at Valenciennes and retreat north-

ward. Stubborn British resistance has been overcome in Calais. Communication between Calais and the main B. E. F. was broken some days ago. It will later be reported that only 30 of the city's 4,000 defenders survived to be evacuated by British naval vessels. A War Office communiqué on May 30 will say of the defense of Calais that it "will count among the most heroic deeds in the annals of the British Army." The French communiqués in general continue not unhopeful. But London admits that the situation in northern France is becoming increasingly grave, and reports that German bombers are attacking Channel shipping and causing serious loss of life.

The French Cabinet meets to discuss the current situation and hear M. Reynaud's report on his visit to London. It is decided to continue the struggle on the Somme and Aisne, and later, if necessary, on the Loire and other rivers further south.

In the evening still worse news for the Allies comes from Belgium. Premier Pierlot has hardly announced over the French radio that the refugee Belgian Cabinet has just met in Paris and unanimously affirmed its will to continue the struggle, when it becomes known to the Allied Governments that, without previously consulting them, King Leopold, as Commander-in-Chief of the Belgian Army, has sent a plenipotentiary to the German Army Headquarters with a request for an armistice. The Belgian Army is already withdrawing from important positions. Premier Pierlot and other Belgian Ministers consult in the evening with Premier Reynaud, Foreign Minister Daladier and General Weygand. A French Cabinet meeting follows and lasts far into the night.

Four workers in French factories are sentenced to death for sabotage, and others engaged in defense activities are arrested for "abandoning work."

As part of the policy aimed at keeping Italy out of the war, London reports that the Allies are preparing to modify their blockade by allowing Italian ships to reach Italy without inspection at contraband control points, in return for which Italy will guarantee that nothing imported into Italy in Italian ships will be reëxported to Germany.

London announces that Sir Stafford Cripps, Laborite member of Parliament, has departed for Moscow as head of an official trade mission, and that the Soviet Government has signified its qualified willingness to receive him.

MAY 28

The German Government refuses King Leopold's request for an armistice. He thereupon accepts the German demand for unconditional surrender. On his orders, the Belgian Army lays down its arms at 4 A.M. It had fought for 18 days.

The Belgian Cabinet meets in Paris at 7 A.M. and unanimously refuses to be associated with King Leopold's action. Premier Reynaud, in a five-minute radio broadcast at 8:30 A.M., hastily arranged after last night's emergency meeting of the French Cabinet, informs the French public of the King's capitulation. He calls the action "without precedent in history" and says that it was taken without warning to General Georges Blanchard, commander of the three allied forces fighting in Belgium. He adds that it is the intention of the Belgian Gov-

ernment to raise a new army to take its place beside the French.
A group of Belgian Senators and Deputies, meeting in Paris,
expresses its disapproval of the King's action. In the evening
Premier Pierlot, in a radio broadcast from Paris, calls the
King's action "illegal and unconstitutional." He points out
that not one Minister has concurred in it, and reaffirms the
Government's decision to continue the struggle. Foreign Minister Spaak, in a press interview, reveals that King Leopold
had decided as long ago as the morning of May 25 to surrender. He says the King reached his decision over the objections of Premier Pierlot and Foreign Minister Spaak, on the
ground that Belgium was bearing the brunt of the German
attack and suffering losses beyond its strength. Before M. Pierlot's speech he and M. Spaak visit the statue of King Albert I
in the Cours la Reine and lay a crêpe-bound wreath at its foot.

The German press praises the courage and independence of
King Leopold, his sense of realism, and his humanity in desir-
ing to spare his country useless suffering.

Prime Minister Churchill, reporting to the House of Commons in the afternoon on the Belgian surrender, emphasizes
that the British and French Armies are entirely disassociated
from that procedure and will "persevere in the operations in
which they are now engaged." He says: "I have no intention
of suggesting to the House that we should attempt at this
moment to pass judgment upon the action of the King of the
Belgians in his capacity as Commander-in-Chief of the Belgian
Army. This Army has fought very bravely and has both in-
flicted and suffered heavy losses." The situation of the British

and French Armies is, he says, "evidently extremely grave,"
and the Commons "should prepare itself for hard and heavy
tidings." But nothing that can happen, declares Mr. Churchill,
can relieve Britain of her duty of defending "the world cause
to which we have vowed ourselves; nor should it destroy our
confidence in our power to make our way—as on former occasions in our history—through disaster and through grief to the
ultimate defeat of our enemies."

The Belgian surrender almost monopolizes the world's attention. But the German High Command reports progress north
of Valenciennes, where there is strong pressure in the direction
of Lille, and speaks of heavy bombing of roads and railways
back of Ostend, Dunkerque and other Channel ports. The
R. A. F. raids German communication lines in that area as
well as military objectives further afield.

MAY 29

Allied troops begin the evacuation of Flanders by sea under
heavy German fire. Ostend has fallen. But the port of Dunkerque remains in Allied possession and small transport vessels
of every sort are gathering to remove the Allied soldiers. Sandy
beaches extend along the coast on either side of Dunkerque.
The waters are shoal for some 12 miles out into the Channel,
and even light-draught vessels must lie at least half a mile from
shore. No warship larger than a destroyer can enter the port
of Dunkerque itself or even approach the jetties that protect it.
Nevertheless, from these beaches and jetties over 300,000 men
are beginning to embark. Back of Dunkerque there is going

on what the London *Times* describes as "a fierce mêlée." Just
to the east, beyond where the River Yser reaches the Channel,
it will report tomorrow that the Germans have advanced
"through silent masses of disarmed Belgians."

The Allies capture Narvik in northern Norway.

President Roosevelt, concerned by the collapse of the Allied
campaign in Flanders, reappraises American defense plans and
decides to ask Congress for $750,000,000 in addition to the
$3,300,000,000 already projected. Secretary Hull modifies the
Neutrality Act restrictions to permit American pilots to deliver
American planes to ports in the eastern Canadian provinces.

MAY 30

Thousands of British and French troops land in England
under the protection of the R. A. F. and the British Navy while
their comrades engage in fierce rear-guard actions against
superior Nazi air and land forces. The perimeter of the Dunkerque defense area is steadily narrowing. Berlin reports the
capture of General Prioux, who had succeeded General Billotte
as commander of the French First Army, and his staff. London announces that new British troops have reached France
and taken up their position on the left flank of the main
French force south of the Somme. (Later information will be
that they number only about a division.) In England further
preparations are in course to resist Germany's advertised invasion, which is recognized to have been rendered much easier
for her by the capture of Holland, Belgium and points on the
French Channel.

The Belgian Cabinet meets in France and approves a decree declaring that "in the name of the Belgian people, in pursuance of Article 32 of the Constitution, and in view of the fact that the King is in the power of the invader . . . it is impossible for the King to reign."

The French Government sends a note to Rome asking for negotiations on outstanding differences, and hinting that it is prepared to go very far to give satisfaction. Mobilization of the Italian Army continues, with 1,500,000 to 1,800,000 men now believed to be under arms.

German civil rule is established in the Netherlands under Dr. Seyss-Inquart, one of the Austrian Ministers who helped arrange their country's annexation to the Reich.

MAY 31

The evacuation of the British forces from Dunkerque continues, with fog aiding the embarkation. London estimates that three-quarters of the British Expeditionary Force have so far been safely evacuated. The German High Command announces that the Flanders and Artois campaigns are virtually over, releasing the German troops in that area "for other tasks." The stage is being set for the second phase of the Battle for France.

The Allied Supreme War Council meets in Paris. Britain is represented by Mr. Churchill, Mr. Attlee, General Dill and others, and France by M. Reynaud, Marshal Pétain, General Weygand and others.

The Belgian Parliament meets at Limoges, France, and

adopts a resolution unanimously expressing indignation at the surrender of King Leopold and describing it as an act for which he will bear a heavy responsibility in history. It repeats the affirmation of the Belgian Cabinet that it is now morally and legally impossible for the King to reign. It proclaims the wish of the Belgians to fight by the side of the Allies until victory has been won. The session is attended by 54 Senators and 89 Deputies.

It is reported from Rome that Mussolini has been so busy with military consultations that he was unable yesterday to receive United States Ambassador Phillips for the presentation of another personal message from President Roosevelt. Presumably it has been delivered to Count Ciano. The French offer to negotiate is rejected, with an intimation that the time for negotiations has passed.

In a special message to Congress, President Roosevelt warns that the conflict may spread to all continents, asks for an additional $1,000,000,000 to supplement defense appropriations, and requests special legislation empowering him to call out the National Guard for active service.

JUNE 1

The embarkation of Allied troops in Flanders is carried forward under increasing difficulties. The Germans take the initiative on the Somme west of Amiens. Berlin predicts a drive into the heart of France and claims that resistance around Lille has been broken and that 26,000 prisoners have been captured. German planes bomb Marseille and industrial centers in the Rhône Valley, killing 46 persons and wounding more than 100.

An official statement issued in London says that the Supreme War Council is in full agreement concerning all the measures required in the situation, and that the two Governments "are more than ever implacably resolved to pursue in the closest possible concord their present struggle until complete victory is achieved." Though the communiqué does not allude to the fact, the Italian situation has been discussed, also relations with Soviet Russia. It has been decided to evacuate Narvik.

Relazioni Internazionali, generally regarded as the organ of the Italian Foreign Office, bluntly declares that Italy is going to intervene with arms against France and Britain. The breaking off of French commercial negotiations with Italy is announced, following the rupture of Anglo-Italian discussions on contraband control.

Grigore Gafencu, pro-Ally Foreign Minister of Rumania, is replaced by Ion Gigurtu, a pro-Nazi.

JUNE 2

Nazi bombers continue their raids down the Rhône Valley, doubtless intended to show Premier Mussolini that Germany is able to support any ventures the Duce might make across the French frontier. Heavy German guns pound Maginot Line positions west of the Moselle, but there is no infantry action.

The evacuation at Dunkerque goes on. War Secretary Anthony Eden, in a brief radio talk, says that the British have saved "more than four-fifths of that B. E. F. which the Germans claimed were surrounded," and calls on his countrymen to work as never before to keep the army supplied.

Prepared to enter the war, Italy is told by Signor Ansaldo, in a broadcast to Italian troops, that "Italy must enter the conflict to keep abreast of the changing times." Articles in the Italian press assume that Italy's claims to Corsica, Bizerta, Nice, Jibuti and Suez can be satisfied only by armed conquest.

Turkish Premier Refik Saydam warns his people they "must not forget that it may be necessary to take up arms to protect this country." London and Paris hope that Italian intervention in the war would result immediately in Turkey's entry.

June 3

A swarm of about 200 German planes drops more than a thousand explosive and incendiary bombs on Paris and its suburbs, killing 254 and injuring 652.

German forces close in on Dunkerque, but Allied troops continue to embark there successfully despite attacks of great ferocity. This is the sixth day of the evacuation. The Germans say that in the Battle of Flanders their casualties are only 10,000 dead and 40,000 wounded.

Count Ciano implies quite clearly to several foreign diplomats that Mussolini's decision to enter the war has already been taken in principle.

June 4

The evacuation from Dunkerque is completed and the town is relinquished to the Germans. At 7 A.M. Admiral Jean Marie

Abrial, commander of the port, clears away in a fast launch. He is the last to leave. There have been house-to-house fighting and hand-to-hand encounters on the beaches and jetties to the very end.

In a long report to the House of Commons, Prime Minister Churchill admits bluntly that the Belgian campaign was a "colossal military disaster." He says that from the moment the Meuse defenses were broken at Sedan "only a rapid retreat to Amiens and the south could have saved the British and French Armies who had entered Belgium at the appeal of the Belgian King, but this strategic fact was not immediately realized." He recapitulates the military results of that failure, describes King Leopold's subsequent surrender of the Belgian Army, and gives a vivid story of the fierce fighting in Calais and Dunkerque and on the Channel and in the air. He acknowledges the enormous loss of material—nearly 1,000 guns and all the transport and armored vehicles of the army in the north—and estimates British dead, wounded and missing at over 30,000. He puts the number rescued at 335,000. Nearly a thousand vessels of all kinds have been used. He pays glowing tribute to the many acts of valor performed, but warns: "Wars are not won by evacuations."

Britain, Mr. Churchill continues, will not be content with a defensive scheme of operations. "We have our duty to our Ally." The B. E. F. will be at once rebuilt. To this end, the defenses in the British Isles must be so perfected "that the largest possible potential of offensive effort may be realized." Mr. Churchill refers with satisfaction to "the solid assurances of sea power" and to Britain's rapidly developing strength in the air. He says he himself has full confidence that "if all do their duty, if nothing is neglected, and if the best arrangements are made, as they are being made, we shall prove ourselves once again able to defend our island home, to ride out the storm of war, and to outlive the menace of tyranny, if necessary for years, if necessary alone." He concludes: "We shall never surrender, and even if, which I do not for a moment believe, this island or a large part of it were subjugated and starving, then our Empire beyond the seas, armed and guarded by the British fleet, would carry on the struggle, until, in God's good time the New World, with all its power and might, steps forth to the rescue and the liberation of the Old."

The Germans estimate that since the start of the Blitzkrieg they have taken a total of 1,200,000 prisoners, which is far in excess of Allied calculations, and that the booty captured is enough to equip 80 divisions, a figure which seems exaggerated. The High Command calls the campaign in Belgium and northern France "the greatest destructive battle of all times," and says its successful conclusion makes certain the "final victory."

In swift reprisal for yesterday's German bombing of Paris, the French and British air forces raid Munich, the Ruhr and Frankfurt.

A neutral estimate of the current situation might be as follows: The result of the successful German drive to the Channel has been to deprive the Allies for the time being of the nine fully trained and equipped divisions of the British Expeditionary Force proper; also of three British territorial divisions sent over mainly for construction work and training behind the front (parts of these were thrown into the fighting around Arras); and of three French Armies (the First, Seventh and Ninth)—a total of perhaps thirty divisions, French and British together. Without these General Weygand has had to form, in the utmost haste, a new front from Abbeville to Montmédy, 165 miles as the crow flies. He has picked up odds and ends of French units from the rear and from other fronts (*e.g.,* the Maginot Line and the Italian frontier), and is utilizing one British division (the 51st) brought over from a quiet sector of the Maginot Line and a new British armored division which is just disembarking. A Canadian division will arrive in Normandy while the Battle of the Somme is in progress, but too late for the actual fighting. It will afterwards be evacuated with difficulty from western ports. So thin is the "Weygand Line" on this date that the single British division now in position on the lower Somme has to hold a frontage of about 24 miles—in other words, it is hardly more than an outpost line.

Premier Reynaud tells the Senate Foreign Affairs Commission that if Italy enters the conflict she will be doing so deliberately for the sole purpose of waging war. Both before and after September 1 the French Government made known to the Italian Government its willingness to find a friendly basis for settling all questions outstanding between the two countries. These overtures met no response. In the past few days they had been renewed, in full accord with the British. Mussolini is well aware, says the French Premier, that the Allies had never closed, and do not now close, the door to any negotiations.

King George sends President Lebrun a message stating that the gallant comradeship in arms shown during the ordeal of the Dunkerque evacuation has revealed to the enemy the full measure of Allied bravery and resolution.

The exchanges between President Roosevelt and Prime Minister Mussolini have been continuing (see May 15, 16, 18 and 31). Mr. Matthews, Rome correspondent of the *New York Times,* notes that the President's message of May 30 was answered a few days later, and that today the President's rejoinder has been received in the Italian capital. The White House confirms that there have been exchanges, and that they are continuing, but authorizes the statement that "not a single true and accurate report on the President's correspondence with Mussolini has yet come from Rome."

The Soviet Union accepts Sir Stafford Cripps as British Ambassador.

A short-wave radio broadcast, heard in London, reports a large-scale demonstration in Barcelona by Spanish students shouting "Gibraltar is Spanish."

Prime Minister Mackenzie King informs the Canadian House of Commons that in the present emergency Canada has placed all her military, naval and air forces completely at the disposal of the British Government.

CHAPTER V

THE BATTLE OF THE SOMME

JUNE 5

At 4 A.M. on a front more than a hundred miles long, from the Channel to near Laon, the Germans launch their second major offensive in the West. Paris is the avowed objective. By some it is called the Battle of the Somme, by others the Battle of France.

In an Order of the Day from Field Headquarters, Chancellor Hitler thanks his soldiers for winning "the greatest battle in the world's history" and announces that "today another great battle begins on the Western Front." He says that "this fight for the freedom and existence of our people now and in the future will be continued until the enemy rulers in London and Paris . . . are annihilated." In a proclamation to the German people, Hitler says that the greatest battle of all times has been brought to a victorious conclusion and that the danger of an invasion of the Ruhr territory has been definitely prevented. He orders flags to be flown for eight days and bells to be rung for three days.

General Weygand's Order of the Day announces that the Battle of France has begun, and that "the order is to defend our positions without thought of retirement." He says: "Cling to our soil, and look only forward; in the rear the High Command has made the necessary dispositions to support you." A communiqué issued after M. Reynaud has appeared before the Military Commission of the Chamber of Deputies announces that the Premier gave details of the withdrawal from Flanders and said that the French nation "is now more than ever determined to fight with its Allies for the liberty of the world." President Lebrun, replying to yesterday's message from King George, says that England's welcome of the French troops and wounded had provided "a new example of the comradeship between our two peoples."

After several days of discussion, Premier Reynaud decides that in the present critical situation he is justified in ignoring usual diplomatic channels. He therefore himself telephones President Roosevelt this afternoon from a private apartment in the Place du Palais Bourbon, making a personal appeal for more American airplanes.

Certain French publicists are arrested, including Robert Fabre-Luce, Serpeille de Gobineau, Alain Laubreaux, Paul Mouton, and Charles Lesca of *Je Suis Partout*—the only occasion during the war, so far as can be ascertained, when the activities of any important French elements favorable to Fascism or Nazism were interfered with by the French police. Charles Julien Masson, former captain in the French Air Corps, is sentenced to death by a military court, together with three associates, one of them a German "traveling salesman," for operating a spy ring which provided the information that enabled the German Air Force to bombard French airports so accurately in the first phase of the war.

Paris announces that General Eugène Mittelhauser has been appointed to succeed General Weygand as Commander of the Allied forces in the Near East, and that he has arrived in Syria after a visit yesterday in Ankara, where he talked with Turkish staff officers.

Under a ruling prepared by Attorney General Jackson, immediate sale to the Allies of at least 600,000 World War rifles and 2,500 field guns, with ammunition, is permitted.

JUNE 6

News comes early in the morning that Premier Reynaud has reconstituted his Cabinet, following the meeting which began at 11:30 last night at the Elysée Palace. M. Reynaud himself takes over the portfolio of Foreign Affairs from M. Daladier, having previously taken over M. Daladier's earlier post at the War Office. There has been strong criticism of M. Daladier's past record as Minister of Defense in recent sessions of both the Military Commission of the Senate and the Military Commission of the Chamber. Other political holdovers from previous régimes are also dropped, including MM. Albert Sarraut and Anatole de Monzie. M. Yvon Delbos becomes Minister of Education; M. Jean Prouvost, owner of *Paris-Soir,* becomes Minister of Information. General Charles de Gaulle is appointed as Under Secretary in the Ministry of Defense, M. Paul Baudouin as Under Secretary in the Foreign Ministry. Both the latter will become very prominent later. General de Gaulle, a tactician and tank expert, will be leader in London of the "Free Frenchmen" movement. M. Baudouin, later to be Foreign Minister under Marshal Pétain, is a former President of the Banque de l'Indo-Chine.

In the evening broadcast Premier Reynaud, who as a result of the Cabinet shakeup now exercises an exceptional degree of political control, tells the nation that he can give it "reason to hope" that the German drive will be stopped. "The battle," he says, "has hardly begun." In this crisis there is no time to lose debating responsibilities for past errors. "We shall not weaken France by dividing her." He adds an indirect offer to Italy to settle outstanding differences without a conflict. In a passage apparently directed to the United States he declares that all spectators of the Battle of France must comprehend quickly what immense values are at stake because "time is limited."

While this is going on in the French political field, German hammer blows continue at the Allied positions along the Somme. The Allies are driven back on both wings of the 120-mile battle front, giving way near Abbeville and losing the crest of the Chemin-des-Dames. Admitting the German advance along the Channel coast below Abbeville and on the Ailette Canal near Soissons, the French High Command nevertheless calls the situation generally favorable. There has been no important break-through such as occurred in the Battle of the Meuse, and it is claimed that the new strategy of permitting the tanks to penetrate the front and then destroying them is working out successfully. A first-hand description of the battlefront describes it as an "immense hell," with 10,000 German tanks being hurled into the engagement. British planes bomb German troops and supply concentrations behind the front, also strategic rail and road connections and oil depots in conquered Belgium, and make raids deep into Germany.

Prime Minister Churchill, replying to questions in Parliament, says that Britain recognizes the Belgian Government at present established in France as the legal Government of Belgium. He declares that "the unswerving aim" of Britain and France is "to secure for Belgium the effective restoration of her freedom and independence."

Orders are issued in Washington that 50 Curtiss-Wright airplanes just delivered to the Navy be returned to the makers, to be exchanged for later models. It is understood they will go to the Allies.

JUNE 7

The tide of the Somme battle turns in favor of the invaders. The German High Command claims to have broken through the "Weygand Line" at several points. British planes continue their bombing attacks immediately behind the lines and on railheads and oil depots in Belgium and Germany. Nazi bombers, in turn, raid the south and east coasts of England.

The French War Cabinet is reduced from 11 to 8 members: Premier Reynaud, Marshal Pétain and MM. Chautemps, Marin, Ybarnégaray, Mandel, Monnet and Dautry.

An ominous sign that Italian participation in the war is imminent is an order withdrawing Italian shipping from all seas.

Lord Beaverbrook, British Minister of Aircraft Supplies, says a 62 percent speed-up in Britain's aircraft production since May 11 has enabled her to replace all plane losses to date.

JUNE 8

The fourth day of the German offensive on the Somme is decisive. The French have to withdraw along the entire western portion of their line, and at some points in the center. The left wing is penetrated by 200 to 300 tanks that cross the Bresle River and reach Forges-les-Eaux, midway between the Bresle and the Seine, only 20 miles from Rouen and 58 miles from Paris. The French center has fallen back 15 to 20 miles along a 60-mile front south of the Somme. The Germans throw in fresh divisions. No fresh French troops are available.

The German success in the Battle of the Somme further encourages Italian interventionists and whets the country's appetite for a share in the prospective booty. Some anxiety is shown about future American policy toward the war, but the prevalent newspaper opinion is that even if the United States should decide to intervene it will do so too late.

Sir Samuel Hoare, new British Ambassador to Spain, presents his credentials at Madrid, and says he finds much in common between Britain and Spain. General Franco replies that he appreciates the choice of Sir Samuel as Ambassador, for he showed a friendly and understanding attitude during National Spain's critical period. Street crowds exploit the occasion to shout "Gibraltar is Spanish!"

A spokesman of the Allied Purchasing Commission in the

United States says that 8,000 planes have been ordered to date, and more than 2,000 delivered.

JUNE 9

The Germans widen their front of attack to the east and open an offensive in great force from Rethel to the Argonne. Some observers say it is the greatest mechanized action of the war. This advance threatens the rear zones of the French armies in the Maginot Line. Further west, the German intention is evidently to advance down the valley of the Marne towards Paris.

In a general order to all troops issued at 10 A.M., an hour after the German attack has begun in the Argonne, General Weygand says: "The enemy has suffered considerable losses. Soon he will reach the end of his effort. This is the last quarter-hour. Hold fast." He predicts that tomorrow the front of attack will extend all the way to Switzerland. Reports in Paris are that the French troops on the new front are resisting and have counter-attacked. But since the collapse on the Somme all the news reaching French General Headquarters is delayed and confused, resulting in communiqués that are already out of date before they can be distributed. At a Cabinet meeting preparations are made to quit Paris. It is the last held in the capital. An exodus of civilians begins.

In the western sector of the front, meanwhile, German motorized units thrust forward to the Seine and reach the outskirts of Rouen. Southwest of Beauvais they reach Gisors, 35 miles from Paris. The French center also is being roughly treated. One thrust carries the Germans across the Aisne on either side of Soissons. Approximately 2,000,000 Germans are estimated to be taking part along the whole line in what the French term an "all-or-nothing" drive for Paris.

The German High Command announces the sinking of the British aircraft carrier *Glorious,* a British destroyer, a 21,000-ton transport, a naval tanker and a submarine chaser in an engagement in the North Sea.

The war in Norway comes to an end as King Haakon and Norwegian Prime Minister Nygaardsvold issue an order to the forces in the north to cease hostilities at midnight. Their proclamation, broadcast by Foreign Minister Koht from Tromsö, Norway, states that the hard necessities of war have forced the Allies to concentrate all their strength on other fronts, and explains that the Norwegian troops have not enough ammunition or combat planes to continue the struggle alone. (Early tomorrow morning, June 10, the Norwegian Government will announce that the Allied forces have withdrawn from Narvik and that King Haakon has arrived in England.)

The Allied Purchasing Commission in the United States announces that, thanks to the ruling in Washington regarding the release of surplus government equipment and material, the flow of muntions of all kinds exported to Europe will be immediately increased.

JUNE 10

The German invaders move closer to Paris, and at one point—south of Beauvais—they are said to be within 25 miles of their goal. A semi-circle has been thrown around the capital from which three wedges are being driven forward. On the French left, one drive carries the Germans across the lower Seine at several points. In the center they press through to the Ourcq valley. The third push is east of Reims.

Prime Minister Churchill telegraphs Premier Reynaud that "the maximum possible support is being given by British forces" in the battle in which the French armies are now so courageously engaging; that "all available means are being used to give help on land, sea, and in the air;" that the Royal Air Force has been constantly engaged over the battle area; and that during the last few days fresh British troops have landed in France to join those already engaged in the common fight, "whilst further extensive reënforcements are being rapidly organized and will shortly be available."

Today, exactly one month after the Nazi invasion of the Low Countries, Fascist Italy enters the war. Foreign Minister Ciano sends for M. François-Poncet, the French Ambassador, at 4:30 P.M. and hands him a note stating, "His Majesty the King and Emperor declares that from tomorrow, June 11, Italy considers herself at war with France." Fifteen minutes later a similar communication is made to Sir Percy Loraine, the British Ambassador. Italy's declaration of war is to become effective at 12:01 A.M., Rome time. At 6 P.M., before a crowd that packs the Piazza Venezia and adjacent streets, Premier Mussolini declares that "this is the hour of irrevocable decisions," announces that the declaration of war has already been handed to the British and French Ambassadors, and says that Italy is going to war against "the plutocratic and reactionary democracies of the West, who have hindered the advance and often threatened the existence even of the Italian people." He solemnly declares that "Italy does not intend to drag other peoples who are her neighbors into this conflict. Let Switzerland, Jugoslavia, Turkey, Egypt, and Greece take note of these words of mine, for it will depend entirely upon them if they are fully confirmed or not."

Hitler telegraphs to King Victor Emmanuel III saying that, "Providence has willed that, against our own intentions, we are compelled to defend the freedom and future of our peoples against Great Britain and France," and expressing the certainty that Germany and Italy will "win a victory . . . and then the vital rights of our two nations will be secure for all time." He telegraphs to the Duce declaring that he is "deeply moved" by the world-historic decision just announced. He says that in September, Great Britain had declared war on Germany without reason. "The increasing contempt for vital national rights by those in power in London and Paris has led us together," he says, "in the great fight for the freedom and future of our countries."

Two hours after the Mussolini speech Premier Reynaud broadcasts a message of defiance and encouragement to the French people. "France," he says, "has gone through still rougher tests and has, at such times, always drawn strength for victory. France cannot die." He claims that enemy gains have been made at the cost of heavy losses in tanks and planes.

"The times ahead are hard, but we are ready, and heads will not be bowed." The French Premier recalls how both he and his predecessors have attempted to settle questions between France and Italy by friendly negotiation; but "Mussolini decided that blood should flow," and on the declaration of war which he has now made "the world that looks at us will judge."

A communiqué issued at Paris in the evening says that Premier Reynaud has gone to visit the armies and that at the request of the High Command the Ministers have left Paris for "the provinces." Some left last night following the Cabinet meeting. Their destination, not yet announced publicly, is Tours. Already the Army Headquarters has been transferred from La Ferté-sous-Jouarre (between Château-Thierry and Meaux) to Briare, on the Loire, about a hundred miles south of Paris.

Across the Atlantic the Italian declaration of war has repercussions also. Prime Minister Mackenzie King, speaking in the Canadian House of Commons, denounces Premier Mussolini as "a carrion bird of prey waiting for brave men to die," and then moves a resolution asking Parliament's approval of a declaration of war against Italy. It is adopted with only one dissenting vote.

After listening to a radio translation of Mussolin's speech, Secretary Hull at his press conference expresses the "deliberate opinion" that Italy's entry into the war "is a great disappointment to peoples everywhere and a great human tragedy." Senator Pittman, Chairman of the Senate Committee on Foreign Relations, declares that it will accelerate American efforts to aid the Allies with "every possible resource short of man-power."

President Roosevelt, in a broadcast speech delivered at 7:15 P.M. (daylight time) before the University of Virginia, at Charlottesville, discusses the philosophy of force which has been adopted by certain countries in Europe and terms it a threat to the American way of life. He describes in some detail his correspondence with Signor Mussolini and reveals that he offered to act as intermediary in transmitting to the British and French Governments any suggestions that the Italian Government might have for securing readjustments which would preserve peace in the Mediterranean area. "Unfortunately," he says, "to the regret of all of us, and to the regret of humanity, the Chief of the Italian Government was unwilling to accept the procedure suggested, and he has made no counter-proposal." The President adds: "On this tenth day of June, 1940, the hand that held the dagger has stuck it into the back of its neighbor." Mr. Roosevelt says that "the whole of our sympathies lies with those nations that are giving their life-blood" in the struggle against "the gods of force and hate." And he says: "We will extend to the opponents of force the material resources of this nation; and at the same time, we will harness and speed up the use of those resources in order that we ourselves in the Americas may have equipment and training equal to the task of any emergency and every defense. All roads leading to the accomplishment of these objectives must be kept clear of obstructions. We will not slow down or detour. Signs and signals call for speed—full speed ahead."

A personal message from Premier Reynaud to President Roosevelt, transmitted through Ambassador Bullitt, is received in Washington at 10:13 P.M. M. Reynaud expresses his gratitude to the President for "the generous aid" he has decided to give in planes and armament on the basis of a previous appeal (*cf.* June 5). After mentioning the "crushing superiority" of the German Army, both in numbers and material, and saying that "today the enemy is almost at the gates of Paris," Premier Reynaud declares: "We shall fight in front of Paris; we shall fight behind Paris; we shall close ourselves in one of our provinces to fight; and if we should be driven out of it we shall establish ourselves in North Africa to continue the fight, and if necessary in our American possessions." He says that France will not abandon the struggle although "this very hour another dictatorship has stabbed France in the back." These words are almost identical with a sentence spoken by President Roosevelt at Charlottesville a few hours earlier. The similarity may perhaps be accounted for by the fact that before sending his formal message M. Reynaud is believed to have again talked over the telephone with Mr. Roosevelt from a private apartment in Paris. The French Premier goes on to declare that it is now his duty to ask the President for "new and even larger assistance," beseeching him "to declare publicly" and "before it is too late" that "the United States will give the Allies aid and material support by all means 'short of an expeditionary force." Recalling President Roosevelt's words on

October 5, 1937, about the peace, freedom and security of 90 percent of the people of the world being jeopardized by the remaining 10 percent, he declares that "the hour has now come" for the 90 percent "to make their will prevail." (The text of the message will be made available in Washington for publication on June 14.)

Chapter VI

THE FRENCH GOVERNMENT AT TOURS

June 11

THE FRENCH FIGHT bitterly to prevent the Germans from spanning the Seine with pontoon bridges which would provide crossings for major units. But the Seine defenses already have been penetrated in some places, and through one such gap the Germans push an advance motorized detachment to the western outskirts of Paris. French military authorities take over charge of the city, and gates and streets are barricaded in preparation for house-to-house fighting. The city is under a pall of smoke from fires in the suburbs, supposedly set by German bombers, and surrounding roads are clogged with fleeing refugees. But officials say that though Paris may be destroyed she will never be surrendered.

The French lines of defense break all along the Marne under fierce German tank and airplane assaults, and the main body of French troops takes up new positions south of the river.

In the east the French also are under tremendous pressure, the German objective being to break the "hinge" where the fluid front from the Channel to Montmédy joins the Maginot Line. In the Channel region, Havre has again been bombed and Allied shipping sunk or damaged.

The French Government reaches Tours. Foreign diplomats and refugees pour into the city; the population quadruples within a few hours. Premier Reynaud arrives in Tours after an overnight visit to the front. He has stopped on the way back for a meeting with the French military chiefs at their new headquarters at Briare. His own headquarters are established near Tours in an old château lacking most of the facilities for serving efficiently as a center of government. The dislocation of government services due to the withdrawal from the capital is much greater than had been anticipated. Conditions in Tours border on the chaotic.

Prime Minister Churchill, Mr. Eden, General Dill and other British official go by air from England to consult with Premier Reynaud, General Weygand and Marshal Pétain. They remain at Tours for further consultations tomorrow.

In the absence of Prime Minister Churchill, Mr. Attlee makes a statement in Parliament on the British Government's attitude towards the Italian declaration of war. He says that hardly ever before in history could a decision to embroil a great nation in conflict have been taken so wantonly and with so little excuse. Britain and France have repeatedly attempted to come to some agreement with Italy to prevent the extension of the war, and they have been patient under constant abuse. Mr. Attlee accuses Premier Mussolini of having declared war for completely sordid motives, seeing an opportunity of securing spoils cheaply at the expense of the western democracies. He uses the analogy of the jackal which tries to obtain some scraps from another beast's kill and of the petty sneak-thief who robs the pockets of a murderer's victim. But Mussolini has made a profound mistake, he says, and the Italians will find that they have to deal with most determined resistance.

The French Finance Minister gives instructions for the seizure of all Italian holdings in France, personal and corporate, and prohibits all transactions with Italy. The police are rounding up Italian fifth column suspects, especially in Marseille and elsewhere in southern France. Anti-Italian demonstrations occur in various places. In England about 1,600 Italians are detained during the day.

Italian planes bomb the British naval base at Malta—the first act of Italian belligerency. They also attack Aden, in an attempt to cut British communications in the Red Sea. The Royal Air Force in turn bombs air fields in Libya and Eritrea. The Franco-Italian frontier is the scene of light skirmishes only.

As a result of Italy's entry into the war, President Roosevelt proclaims the Mediterranean Sea a combat zone, and closes it to American ships, airplanes and citizens.

JUNE 12

The German High Command reports that "full success" has now crowned the operations begun June 5 along the Somme front from the English Channel to a point south of Laon. After recapitulating German successes, the communiqué says the German troops are now approaching Paris on three sides. At the nearest point they are only 12½ miles distant from the capital. Berlin says Rouen has been in German hands "for several days," and announces the capture of Reims; but the French concede only that the latter is under attack. In the coastal region below Dieppe, the Germans speak of capturing an Allied force of 20,000 men, including six generals, along with "vast quantities" of war materials. This, they say, opens the way for a drive towards Havre.

From Tours, the French Government admits that the enemy has reached the "outworks of Paris" and reveals that the Marne has been crossed by the enemy between Meaux and Château-Thierry. But high officials, both military and civilian, know that their information is scrappy and out of date. Communication with the troops that have been engaged in intense fighting is suffering badly from the fact that there is no longer any real "front" in the accepted sense of the word. Local commanders are being forced to deal with current emergencies on their own responsibility. In some cases, it seems, the general discouragement and disorder following the collapse on the Somme and the Marne and the abandonment of Paris are leading individual officers and groups of men to start for "home." In the eastern section of the front, however, the hinge of the Maginot Line at Montmédy still holds.

Tours is bombed by German planes. Mr. Churchill and his colleagues confer again this morning with M. Reynaud, Marshal Pétain and General Weygand, and return to London. They have received black reports on the military position and are disturbed by the French political situation. But the communiqué issued later in London, after Mr. Churchill has seen King George, is indefinite, merely stating that "complete agreement was reached as to the measures to be taken to meet developments in the war situation." Lord Lloyd, Colonial Minister, also goes back to England after seeing various French ministers.

The French Cabinet meets at the Château de Cangé, about ten miles outside Tours, and hears from General Weygand that the military situation is desperate, and that he believes there is no longer any hope of preventing the German occupation of all France. The question arises of asking for an armistice. General Weygand says that for military reasons it is highly advisable. Passing somewhat outside the realm of his military competence, he adds the argument that peace must be made at once, before the appearance of the social disorders which he considers imminent. He allegedly alarms the Cabinet and President Lebrun by saying he has just been informed that Maurice Thorez, Communist leader, is already installed in the Elysée Palace. But M. Mandel, who as Minister of the Interior is responsible for the maintenance of public order, is able to confirm, by telephoning to M. Langeron, Préfet of Paris, that the city is quiet and that there has been no Communist uprising. The general conclusion of the Cabinet is that in view of General Weygand's advice Mr. Churchill should be asked to visit Tours again for further discussions aiming to relieve France of her obligation not to make a separate peace. (A statement issued in Bordeaux by Propaganda Commissioner Prouvost on June 24, *q.v.*, will state merely that "the predominating opinion" in the Cabinet on this date was that "France, with or without an armistice, could not escape total occupation," and that Mr. Churchill should return "for consultation.")

The obligation not to make a separate peace, referred to above, was assumed by each of the two nations under the Anglo-French Agreement adopted at the sixth meeting of the Allied Supreme War Council in London on March 28. At that time the two Governments agreed to a "solemn declaration," as follows: "The Government of the French Republic and His Majesty's Government in the United Kingdom of Great Britain and Northern Ireland mutually undertake that during the present war they will neither negotiate nor conclude an armistice or treaty of peace except by mutual agreement. They undertake not to discuss peace terms before reaching complete agreement on the conditions necessary to ensure to each of them an effective and lasting guarantee of their security. Finally, they undertake to maintain, after the conclusion of peace, a community of action in all spheres for so long as may be necessary to safeguard their security and to effect the reconstruction, with the assistance of other nations, of an international order which will ensure the liberty of peoples, respect for law, and the maintenance of peace in Europe."

British planes bomb Genoa, Milan and Turin. These raids, repeated frequently in succeeding days, give the Italian population its first taste of modern warfare.

Turkey severs commercial relations with Italy, orders all her ships to proceed immediately to the nearest Turkish port to await instructions, and is reported to be sending her battle fleet through the Sea of Marmora towards the Dardanelles. The

Government is thought to await a hint from Russia before making a decision between war and peace. Doubtless it also is watching military events in France with close attention. In the evening the Turkish Cabinet meets and decides to stay out of the war at present, but to redouble defensive preparations. But the Government emphasizes that Turkey is not retreating from her pledge to go to the aid of the Allies in the event of aggression leading to full war in the Mediterranean area.

The Egyptian Government severs diplomatic relations with Italy. It intimates that a state of war will automatically ensue if Egyptian soil is attacked by air, land or sea.

The new British and French Ambassadors to Soviet Russia, Sir Stafford Cripps and M. Erik Labonne, arrive in Moscow. Signor Augusto Rosso, Italian Ambassador to Russia, also arrives back at his post. The Russian Ambassador to Italy, Ivan Gorelkin, is en route to Italy, marking the resumption of normal diplomatic relations between Rome and Moscow. Mr. Gorelkin left Rome last December, before he had presented his credentials, following Italian student demonstrations against Russia, then at war with Finland.

Eighty additional United States Army attack bombers are released for use by the Allies as the President's orders for "full speed ahead" in efforts to aid "the opponents of force" begin to produce results (*cf.* June 6). The House passes and sends to the Senate a $1,706,053,908 supplemental defense appropriation. The President signs the $1,308,171,000 Naval Appropriation Bill.

June 13

With the Germans in the outskirts of Paris on three sides, Ambassador Bullitt, acting at the request of General Dentz, Commander of the Paris area, transmits to the German Government formal notice that the capital has been declared an open city and that the defending army is being withdrawn. Mr. Bullitt, who has found himself almost without communication with the outside world since the French Government moved to Tours, is able to forward General Dentz's message to Berlin as a result of an unexpected telephone call which comes through this morning from the American Legation in Berne. The object is to spare Paris from destruction. Notices that the capital has been declared an open city are posted in public places. The Préfet orders the police to stay at their posts; the firemen also remain. Mr. Bullitt has decided that he should remain in Paris, with the principal members of the Embassy staff, in the hope of arranging that the transfer of the city administration to the Germans take place without loss of life.

Meanwhile motorized and armored German columns are pouring over the Seine bridges between Rouen and Paris, especially at Louviers, Les Andelys and Vernon. Towns further west, including Dreux and Evreux, are heavily bombed. North of the city, in the neighborhood of Senlis, at least twelve German divisions are closing in. Further east the enemy has crossed the Marne just above Château-Thierry, and still further east is at Châlons-sur-Marne. The forces thrown into the attack between the Seine and the Meuse are estimated to total 100 divisions as a minimum. The German left wing is threatening to turn the Maginot Line.

An official British statement announces that south of the Seine fresh British troops have taken their place in the line with the French, and that additional troops and material are on the way. This refers evidently to the residual units already on the Continent, but which were outside the German sweep into Flanders, and certain new units hurried across the Channel (*cf.* June 4). British planes continue to be very active, and give a good account of themselves in encounters with the superior enemy air forces.

The French Cabinet gathers at 3 P.M. and considers further the possibility of requesting Germany for an armistice. It suggests that Prime Minister Churchill, who has returned to Tours, should meet with them to discuss the whole question. He declines to be put in such a false position. Instead, he talks with the French Prime Minister, also with M. Georges Mandel, Minister of the Interior (Clemenceau's former associate, and like Clemenceau always a partisan of strong resistance to Germany). Afterwards he starts back again for London. He has been accompanied on this trip by Lord Halifax, Foreign Secretary, and Lord Beaverbrook, Minister of Aircraft Production. At 5 P.M MM. Reynaud and Mandel carry to the French Cabinet the information that they have seen Mr. Churchill and the other British Ministers, and that these have now left for home.

According to the French version (published by M. Prouvost, High Commissioner for Propaganda, at Bordeaux, June 24, *q.v.*), M. Reynaud's report to the Cabinet is as follows: "The British Premier, in accord with Lord Halifax and Lord Beaverbrook, who accompanied him to France, declared that the British Government will continue to give France, as in the past, the maximum military, air and naval support in its power; but that if events force France to demand an armistice from Germany, the opinion of Churchill, Halifax and Beaverbrook was that England in no event would heap blame on her ally in trouble and would understand the situation in which France found herself, much against her will." This version adds that M. Reynaud's statement was made in the presence of M. Baudouin, Under-Secretary of State for Foreign Affairs, subsequently Minister of Foreign Affairs in the Pétain Cabinet. It continues: "The decision to ask for an armistice was again put off 24 hours for two reasons: first, to await President Roosevelt's reply to France's supreme appeal and, second, to give the London Cabinet more precise information regarding the situation and the apparent consequences." And the accusation is added that in the meantime "certain French Ministers, notably Georges Mandel, acting without government instructions, intervened with the British Government so that the Churchill, Beaverbrook and Halifax declarations could not be maintained and so that Britain could take toward France a much less comprehensive and a more imperative attitude."

The British version (presented by Mr. Churchill in Parliament June 25) is that the invitation to come to Tours had been made directly to him by M. Reynaud "when it became clear that the defeat and subjugation of France was imminent, and that her fine Army on which so many hopes were set was reeling under the German flail." At this meeting, according to Mr. Churchill, Mr. Reynaud, "after dwelling on the conditions at the front and the state of the French Army," asks him "whether Great Britain would release France from her obligation not to negotiate for an armistice or peace without the consent of her British ally. Although I knew how great French sufferings were, and that we had not so far endured equal trials or made an equal contribution in the field, I felt bound to say that I could not give consent. . . . We agreed that a further appeal should be made by M. Reynaud to the United States, and that if the reply was not sufficient to enable M. Reynaud to go on fighting—and he, after all, was the fighting spirit—then we should meet again and take a decision in the light of the new factors."

The two versions, it will be noted, coincide in stating that the French Cabinet, which has already half-way made up its mind to ask for an armistice, consents to postpone action pending a reply to an appeal to be made by M. Reynaud to President Roosevelt. The French omits any reference to an agreement that if the response is inadequate there shall be another Anglo-French consultation before decisive action is taken.

In a broadcast at 11:30 in the evening Premier Reynaud announces that he has sent President Roosevelt "a new and final appeal"—evidently in accordance with the procedure cited above. He calls for "clouds of war planes" to come across the Atlantic "to crush the evil force that dominates Europe." He says that each time he has asked Mr. Roosevelt to increase the assistance permitted under American law, the President has generously complied and the American people have approved. After declaring that wounded France "has the right to turn to other democracies and to say: 'We have claims on you'," M. Reynaud asks whether the American people will "hesitate still to declare themselves against Nazi Germany." The Premier asserts that "despite our reverses the power of the democracies remains immense." Declaring that "the world must know of the sufferings of France," he says the hour has come for it to pay its debt. He declares ominously that "our fight, each day more painful, has no further sense if in continuing we do not see even far away the hope of a common victory growing." He concludes: "In the great trials of their history our people have known days when they were troubled by defeatist counsel. It is because they never abdicated that they were great. No matter what happens in the coming days, the French are going to suffer. May they be worthy of the past of the nation. May they become brothers. May they unite about their wounded fatherland. The day of resurrection will come!"

After word comes from Tours quoting Premier Reynaud as saying that he has sent Mr. Roosevelt a "final appeal," Stephen T. Early, White House Secretary, authorizes correspondents to say that the text of the Premier's statement has not yet been received, but that "everything possible is being done to forward supplies to France." (And in actual fact, in the confusion which prevails at Tours, the text of the appeal has not yet been put on the wires, and will not be until tomorrow morning.)

Late in the evening the British Government dispatches a message to the French Government paying high tribute to the heroism and constancy of the French Army in its battle against enormous odds. It says it takes "this opportunity of proclaiming the indissoluble union of our two peoples and our two Empires." It continues: "We cannot measure the various forms of tribulation which will fall upon our peoples in the near future. We are sure that the ordeal by fire will only fuse them together into one unconquerable whole. We renew to the French Republic our pledge and resolve to continue the struggle at all costs in France, in this island, upon the oceans, and in the air, wherever it may lead us, using all our resources to the utmost limits, and sharing together the burden of repairing the ravages of war. We shall never turn from the conflict until France stands safe and erect in all her grandeur, until the wronged and enslaved States and peoples have been liberated, and until civilization is free from the nightmare of Nazidom. That this day will dawn we are more sure than ever. It may dawn sooner than we now have a right to expect."

For the third time since the beginning of the war Generalissimo Franco announces that Spain is remaining outside the conflict. But the decree published in Madrid differs from previous statements in proclaiming Spain's "non-belligerency" instead of "neutrality."

JUNE 14

Paris falls. Ambassador Bullitt expected the German troops yesterday, but the first detachment which presented itself at the Porte de Pantin, in the northwest corner of the city, was fired on by an irresponsible French soldier and withdrew. The occupation was delayed until today, when soon after 7 A.M. the first motorcyclists enter the capital. They are followed by German cameramen, radio technicians and announcers, who station themselves in the Place de la Concorde to record the scene as German troops pass through the center of the city. It is a sunny morning. The swastika floats from the Arc de Triomphe and from the Eiffel Tower.

According to a German version published August 12, Nazi officers yesterday sent an "open message over the radio" offering to treat Paris as a non-belligerent zone if the city would surrender at once. They then attempted to get in touch with the French occupying forces under a flag of truce. But the effort failed when the German delegation was fired on by mistake by French Senegalese troops. At 6 A.M. today French delegates arrive at the village of Ecouen, some 10 miles from Paris on the road to Chantilly, and begin negotiations with German officers regarding the conditions for the surrender and occupation of Paris. The French in general accept the conditions of the German High Command, but raise a question as to what area constitutes Paris. They explain that they are empowered to surrender only the city proper and not its environs. Under threats that a concentric attack with artillery of the heaviest calibers will begin at once if the German demand is not accepted, the French signature is affixed to the protocol of surrender. At about 7:45 A.M. armored cars, tanks and infantry advance into Paris from the northwest, passing through

Neuilly and following the Champs Elysées into the heart of the city.

The Parisians stand grimly on the curb as Germans march through their boulevards for the first time since 1871. It is the ninth recorded invasion of Paris. Only a third of the citizens remain. Shops are closed and shuttered. The police and civil guards remain on duty but surrender their arms.

In Berlin the fall of Paris provokes scenes of wild rejoicing. On Chancellor Hitler's orders church bells are rung and the Nazi flag is ordered displayed for three days. Berlin describes the event as "catastrophic" morally and economically for the French and says it completes the second phase of the war. The first was the Battle of Flanders. The third will be the pursuit and "final destruction" of all the French forces.

The major objective of the Germans in this third and "final" phase of the war is evidently going to be to turn the flank of the Maginot Line by pressing straight south from the Argonne through Champagne. Montmédy, westernmost fort of the Line, has already been taken; and the German advance now reaches Vitry-le-François, threatening Verdun and Nancy. They also open an artillery attack on the Maginot Line in the region of the Saar. On the Channel they claim to be in Havre and to be advancing down the coast towards Cherbourg.

The French High Command says Paris was abandoned because there was no valid strategic reason why it should be defended and in order to avoid its destruction. The communiqué says that the French Army is retreating in good order. Military circles admit that the rapid German advance in

Champagne threatens the Maginot Line, as its guns are useless against an attack from the rear.

The French Government moves from Tours to Bordeaux. Before leaving Tours by car about noon Premier Reynaud arranges to dispatch to Washington the text of the appeal referred to in last night's broadcast. The text of this appeal (which is not made public) corresponds in part to the radio speech itself, but is even more urgent and dramatic. It is transmitted via Ambassador Biddle, who calls at the Premier's château about 9:30 A.M. to inquire about it. The British are incensed when they hear that M. Reynaud has implied in this message that if France is forced to withdraw from the war they will not be able to continue the struggle alone with any hope of success.

In an interview with Karl von Wiegand, chief foreign correspondent for the Hearst newspapers, Chancellor Hitler seeks to offset the French appeals for increased American help. He says that his policy is "Europe for the Europeans and America for the Americans." He denounces as a lie the idea that he has ever dreamed of interfering with affairs in the Western Hemisphere, describing American fears on that score as childish and grotesque. He also denies that he wants to smash the British Empire, but says he will simply destroy those who are destroying that Empire. He asserts that in any event American assistance will not affect the outcome of the war, and hence that American policy is not his affair and really does not interest him. As for his more remote aims, he tells Mr. von Wiegand he has only one—peace. Informed of the von Wiegand story, Mr. Roosevelt remarks at a press conference: "That brings up recollections."

In London it is stated in government circles that Britain has agreed to accept whatever military and political decisions France feels she must make, provided they are preceded by full and frank consultation. If France is lost as an ally, Britain will continue the struggle alone.

Prime Minister Mackenzie King reads to the Canadian House of Commons the communication sent last night by the British Government to the French Government, as also a message which he has sent today to M. Reynaud declaring that "Canada pledges to France as she has to Britain her unwavering support to the utmost limit of her power and resources."

CHAPTER VII

THE FRENCH REQUEST FOR AN ARMISTICE

JUNE 15

GERMAN TROOPS PENETRATE with amazing speed into central France. One German spearhead reaches Chaumont, 50 miles up the Marne from Vitry-le-François, reported yesterday as just captured. Verdun falls, and further east the Germans cross the Rhine into Alsace. Berlin says 200,000 prisoners have been taken in the past ten days. The swastika flies over the Palace of Versailles.

The Italians report that they have launched two drives into France, one north of Nice, the other through difficult Alpine passes into Savoy. This is the first Italian military activity of any importance. It begins as the power of the French to defend themselves has already come nearly to an end. Even so, Italian military accomplishments in this area will be negligible.

President Roosevelt discusses the Reynaud appeal with the French and British Ambassadors, Count de Saint-Quentin and Lord Lothian. They call at the White House at noon, and the conference lasts about an hour. The possibilities of continued French resistance outside France proper and the future of the French fleet are two of the questions coming under review. The two Ambassadors urge the President to make his reply public, but receive no promise to that effect. The intimation at the State Department yesterday was that it would not be published. Soon after they leave, however, the text is given out. In it the President pledges redoubled efforts to supply all possible moral and material assistance "so long as the Allied Governments continue to resist." He writes: "I believe it is possible to say that every week that goes by will see additional matériel on its way to the Allied nations." In accordance with the American Government's policy of not recognizing "the results of conquest of territory acquired through military aggression," he says that it "will not consider as valid any attempts to infringe by force the independence and territorial integrity of France." The President's message concludes: "I know that you will under-stand that these statements carry with them no implication of military commitments. Only the Congress can make such commitments."

British officials issue a denial of reports that the French con-template making a separate peace. The Foreign Office asserts that stories of a disagreement between the British and French civil and military authorities are "completely devoid of foun-dation," and that the Allies will continue, as hitherto, in close consultation and complete agreement. No effort is made to minimize the critical nature of the military situation, but it is said flatly that intimations of an imminent French surrender or collapse have no basis in fact. The war will continue, no matter what blows Germany may strike, no matter what losses the Allies may suffer.

The French Cabinet meets in the evening in Bordeaux. The

session, which lasts 3½ hours, is presided over by President Lebrun and attended by General Weygand, Admiral Jean Darlan, French naval chief, and General Joseph Vuillemin, Chief of Staff of the French Air Force. Another session is announced for tomorrow.

After several days of intensive consultation with the British and French Ambassadors, the Turkish Government decides that for the present it will continue its attitude of non-belligerency.

The Spanish Government announces that it has occupied the International Zone at Tangier "provisionally," in order to guarantee its neutrality.

Soviet troops occupy Lithuania after a Russian ultimatum that the Lithuanian Government resign in favor of one which is pro-Communist.

Colonel Charles A. Lindbergh returns to the air in another address on the international situation. He criticizes the Administration for "making gestures with an empty gun after we have already lost the draw," and says there are "men among us" who "have baited the trap of war with requests for modest assistance."

JUNE 16

This Sunday is a decisive date in French history. The French Cabinet has three meetings in the Prefecture at Bordeaux. In fact, it is in almost continuous session. While these meetings are going on, Premier Reynaud is several times in communication with London, sometimes *via* the British Ambassador, Sir Ronald Campbell, sometimes directly over the telephone with

General de Gaulle, French Under-Secretary of War, who happens to be in London on one of his frequent liaison missions for the Reynaud Government. He also talks with M. Herriot and M. Jeanneney, heads respectively of the Chamber and Senate. M. Reynaud has sent word to Mr. Churchill that President Roosevelt's reply to the appeal for fuller and more immediate American help is not satisfactory, and has renewed his demand that France be released from the obligation not to make a separate peace. The British Government reminds him formally that the obligation depends on an agreement made by the French Republic, not the promise of any single statesman or administration. The British Government nevertheless tells him (as reported by Mr. Churchill in the Commons on June 25) that in view of French sufferings it will give approval to the French Government's engaging in separate armistice negotiations on one condition—namely, that the French fleet be dispatched to British ports and that it remain there while the negotiations are in progress. The British Government makes clear that in any event it is resolved to continue the war, and it repudiates "any association with such enquiries about an armistice." In one of his telephone talks with Bordeaux, General de Gaulle sends word that an important affirmative proposal will be submitted from London later in the day, and he urges M. Reynaud not to allow the Cabinet to make any important decisions in advance of its arrival.

The British proposal, presented to Premier Reynaud about 5 P.M. by Sir Ronald Campbell, the British Ambassador, consists of the draft for an "Act of Union" between Great Britain and France. The idea is not new, but has never been raised before in such concrete form. It is suggested that there shall at once be formed an "indissoluble union" between the two nations, with a Constitution providing for joint organs of defense and the joint conduct of foreign, financial and economic policies. "Every citizen of France will enjoy immediately citizenship of Great Britain, every British subject will become a citizen of France." During the present war there will be a single war cabinet, and all the forces of the two nations on land, sea and air will be placed under its direction. "The two Parliaments will be formally associated." New armies are being raised; and "France will keep her available forces in the field, on the sea, and in the air." The Union will appeal for American aid in strengthening its joint economic resources. "The Union will concentrate its whole energy against the power of the enemy, no matter where the battle may be. And thus we shall conquer." In the course of one of his talks with London about this very sweeping plan M. Reynaud is allegedly told that if it is immediately accepted by the French Government there is a possibility that he can at once become the first head of the new unified war cabinet—in fact, Prime Minister of the Franco-British Union.

M. Reynaud carries the British offer to the Cabinet, which has been discussing President Roosevelt's reply to the "final and supreme" French appeal. That reply is accepted as representing about all that Mr. Roosevelt could promise; but his reference to the power of the American Congress to prevent any military commitment recalls French disappointments over the American Senate's rejection of the Treaty of Versailles, and it is used as a strong argument by the members of the Cabinet who favor prompt surrender. The division in the Cabinet is almost even. Those who favor continuation of the war, if necessary from North Africa, include MM. Mandel, Campinchi, Delbos, Monnet, Marin and Dautry. Some, it will be noted, are Rightists, some are Leftists. They are supported from outside the Cabinet by MM. Herriot and Jeanneney. Admiral Darlan is also said to wish to continue the war on sea and from Algeria, Tunisia and French Morocco. The opponents of continued resistance are headed by Vice Premier Pétain, who is in accord with General Weygand. They are said to believe, in addition to the other reasons already noted in support of their position, that Britain, too, must soon succumb to the invincible Nazis. Outside the Cabinet, ex-Premier Laval is active in favor of making terms at once. It is accepted in Bordeaux that he is in touch with the Spanish Ambassador, Señor Lequerica, who, it is suggested, might serve as an intermediary in the event the French authorities decided to get into touch with Chancellor Hitler. Several Cabinet members, including M. Chautemps, vacillate. No definite action is taken on the British proposal. The Cabinet adjourns at 7:45 P.M.

When the French Cabinet reassembles about 10 P.M. General Weygand is called in for a final report. There is further discussion of the British offer of union. Some reports say that it is rejected 14–10, others that no formal vote is taken. In any event, a vote is now taken on the proposal to ask Germany for terms. *The Cabinet votes 13 to 11 in favor of an armistice,*

and M. Reynaud resigns. President Lebrun asks Marshal Pé-
tain to form a Government. One report is that he promptly
pulls the list of his Cabinet members out of his pocket; another
is that he goes into an adjoining room to consult President
Lebrun, and that while he is there the ex-Ministers who had
voted for resistance leave the room. In Marshal Pétain's new
Cabinet the Vice Premier is M. Chautemps. General Weygand
becomes Minister of Defense; M. Baudouin, Foreign Minister;
General Louis Colson, Minister of War; Admiral Darlan, Minister of the Navy and Merchant Marine; General Bertrand
Pujo, Minister of Air; M. Ybarnégaray, Minister of War Vet-
erans and Families. By 10:30 M. Reynaud has left the meeting. At 11:30 P.M. the French radio announces that he is out
and that Marshal Pétain heads the new Government. *Mar-*
shal Pétain this same evening sends for Señor Lequerica, the
Spanish Ambassador, and asks that Madrid communicate to
Chancellor Hitler the French Government's request for an
armistice. The Papal Nuncio, Mgr. Valerio Valeri, also par-
ticipates in the negotiations.

News of the overthrow of the French Cabinet comes to
Prime Minister Churchill as he is seated in a train in a London station. M. Reynaud has asked him to come to Bordeaux
for the final consultation agreed upon at Tours on June 13,
and he is about to start. He alights from the train and returns
to 10 Downing Street; and after consulting the Cabinet sends
word to the new Pétain Government reminding it of the formal conditions which the British Government has enjoined
upon the preceding French Government regarding a separate

peace, specifically the guarantees about the French fleet. He points out (according to his June 25 statement) that there still is plenty of time for the Pétain Government to give the necessary orders about the fleet even while starting to get into touch with Berlin. After the emergency meeting of the Cabinet, newspapermen are merely informed that Britain will continue the war under any and all conditions.

General de Gaulle has already started by air for Bordeaux to report about the British offer in more detail. He arrives to find M. Reynaud out of office and the new Cabinet committed to making peace. His friends say that he calls on M. Reynaud at his hotel, salutes, and without any more than a formal interchange of remarks regains his plane and returns to London. He there begins making plans to organize those Frenchmen who wish to continue to fight.

Throughout this day of such momentous political negotiations the German Armies have not stood still. *The Maginot Line, taken in the rear by the German advance, is virtually abandoned.* From Switzerland it is reported that most of the French divisions in the Line have been successfully withdrawn, leaving only small detachments to harass the Germans, and that the French intention seems to be to establish a new defense line across France from the Swiss border to the Loire. But Berlin says that the German armies which are racing towards the Loire have no real contact with the French forces at any point.

Waves of German and Italian bombing planes visit Tours and wreck whole blocks of homes and business houses. The city is crowded with refugees and the dead and injured number several hundreds.

The activity of the Italian Army on the French frontier fails to develop into a major offensive. The Italian air force raids several air bases in southern France. It also bombs Malta for the twentieth time, as well as two Egyptian ports near Libya. The British report four Italian submarines sunk and two bases in Italian East Africa raided. Raids of this sort will from now on be of almost daily occurrence.

Soviet troops occupy Latvia and Estonia.

June 17

Marshal Pétain broadcasts a statement in the morning announcing that he has assumed direction of the Government and declaring that France no longer has the military power to continue the war "against an enemy superior in numbers and in arms." He says: "It is with a heavy heart I say we must cease the fight. I have applied to our opponent to ask him if he is ready to sign with us, as between soldiers after the fight and in honor, means to put an end to hostilities."

At 4:30 P.M. Berlin announces that Chancellor Hitler and Premier Mussolini will at once meet in Munich to discuss what terms to offer France, the strategy of the war against Britain, and policies in the Balkans. In the evening Mussolini sets out, accompanied by Count Ciano. The Berlin radio also makes plain that the French request for negotiations is not a capitulation nor even a formal plea for an armistice; Marshal Pétain's order to cease fire does not portend that an armistice will automatically be concluded. "The pursuit of the French Army," it says, "will continue."

In a broadcast at 9:30 P.M. Foreign Minister Baudouin rectifies the impression given by Premier Pétain that fighting has already ceased. He says that the Government has had to ask for conditions of peace because, although the British fleet has not lost mastery of the seas, and though Britain's troops and "magnificent Air Force" have "shared our battles," forty million Frenchmen are now facing "almost alone" eighty million Germans, plus the Italians. "Modern war cannot be improvised, and our friends have not been able to bring us the support necessary to the advance guard which the French Army represented." But though the Government has had to ask for terms, "they have not abandoned their arms." France is ready to seek an honorable peace. "But she will never be ready to accept shameful conditions which would mean the end of spiritual freedom for her people." And the evening communiqué of the French Army, broadcast by the French radio, affirms that "at all points of contact our troops are still fighting with the same bravery for the honor of the flag."

The fighting is, in fact, continuing in some areas with great stubbornness on the French side. Berlin reports that a German column has penetrated to the French-Swiss border southwest of Besançon and that the Maginot Line in consequence is completely isolated. A desperate fight is put up by the French to keep the foe from crossing the middle Loire. But the French evening communiqué admits that it has been crossed. A flying

German column captures Orléans. In northern Lorraine, German troops are approaching St. Mihiel, and are also advancing through the Maginot Line south of Saarbrücken. Sarrebourg and other cities in that area have been taken, despite strong French resistance. A later German communiqué announces the capture of the fortress of Metz. French military spokesmen in Bordeaux admit to the Associated Press that the Army has been split into four parts. No continuous front is being held. The French radio announces, however, that the French fleet and air force are "intact."

The B.E.F. and members of the Royal Air Force are being withdrawn from France as rapidly as possible. The *S.S. Lancastria,* evacuating troops from St. Nazaire, is sunk this afternoon in the Loire with a loss of over 4,000 lives.

In the evening Prime Minister Churchill broadcasts the following brief message: "The news from France is very bad, and I grieve for the gallant French people who have fallen into this terrible misfortune. Nothing will alter our feelings towards them, or our faith that the genius of France will rise again. What has happened in France makes no difference to British faith and purpose. We have become the sole champions now in arms to defend the world cause. We shall do our best to be worthy of that high honor. We shall defend our island, and, with the British Empire around us, we shall fight on unconquerable until the curse of Hitler is lifted from the brows of men. We are sure that in the end all will be well." The text of yesterday's offer to France of an "Act of Union" is also made public in London. It remains unknown generally in France, due to interference with the transmission of radio news from England.

There have been some other events in Bordeaux during the day which though minor are worth recording. Ex-Premier Reynaud has received a private message from President Roosevelt expressing his personal regret over the fall of the Cabinet and the failure of the policy of resistance. M. Reynaud has replied with an expression of thanks, adding that he realizes the President went to the limit of his powers in offering assistance to France. M. Mandel, until last evening Minister of the Interior, has been arrested while lunching at the Chapon Fin restaurant in Bordeaux. He is released shortly afterwards, however, with apologies, upon urgent representations to Premier Pétain made jointly and in person by M. Herriot, President of the Chamber, and M. Jeanneney, President of the Senate.

On receipt of definite information that the French Government has opened negotiations with Germany, President Roosevelt issues an order "freezing" the assets in the United States of France and her nationals. This will prevent Germany from realizing on those assets, amounting to approximately $1,000,-000,000. In New York, the British Purchasing Commission announces that it is taking over all French war orders.

The United States Senate, by a vote of 76 to 0, adopts a joint resolution declaring that the United States will refuse to recognize change of title from one European Power to another of "any geographic region in the Western Hemisphere." Today also (though announcement will not be made until June 19) Secretary Hull instructs American diplomatic representatives in Berlin and Rome to make the American Government's position in this matter clear to the German and Italian Foreign Ministers. Each of them is told that the United States, having heard of the French request for an armistice, "feels it desirable, in order to avoid any possible misunderstanding, to inform Your Excellency that in accordance with its traditional policy relating to the Western Hemisphere, the United States would not recognize any transfer, and would not acquiesce in any attempt to transfer, any geographic region of the Western Hemisphere from one non-American power to another non-American power." The French, British and Netherland Governments receive similar notices. Thus the United States is committed to oppose any such transfer, whether it be French Guiana or the Dutch West Indies to Germany or Italy, or even Greenland to Great Britain. In preparation for maintaining this position, the United States today sends notes inviting the Foreign Ministers of the other 20 American Republics to meet in emergency session to discuss the new problems in the Western Hemisphere arising from the European war. (Announcement that invitations have been sent for this conference, which meets in Habana July 21, will be made June 19.)

JUNE 18

Despite the French request for an armistice, the Germans press forward in all directions, determined to scourge France until their terms are accepted. After some violent actions, advance German forces enter Cherbourg (77 miles across the Channel from Britain's great naval base at Portsmouth) and

Rennes, capital of Brittany. In the eastern part of the country the Germans claim that the French military collapse proceeds apace, and that their troops have thrust beyond the headwaters of the Loire and south along the Swiss border. Among the cities occupied are Nevers, Dijon, Belfort and Metz. On the upper Rhine, Colmar has been taken.

Chancellor Hitler arrives in Munich at noon, and greets Premier Mussolini when the latter's special train pulls in three hours later. The arrival of the two dictators is heralded with what is reported as "unprecedented jubilation." Their conference opens at the Fuehrer House shortly after 4 and ends at 8:10, when a communiqué is issued stating merely that they have reached "an agreement on the attitude of both Governments toward the French request for an armistice." In a blaze of Nazi and Italian flags and a din of "Heils" and "Vivas" Signor Mussolini entrains for Rome, and shortly afterwards Herr Hitler starts back for his army headquarters. German radio bulletins state that "peace with honor was denied in 1918 to a Germany starved by the blockade," and that Germany's present victory will be based on a stark sense of reality. The war will go on until the political and military system of France is smashed.

There are air raid alarms in Bordeaux. The opinion there, states a Reuter dispatch, is that they are part of the tactics of the Germans to "harry the French Government in a physical way as much as possible in order to obtain the kind of peace they want."

The French radio repeats over and over again that France will accept only honorable conditions of peace and that, pending the German reply, she will continue the struggle. At 6:30 P.M. the French station announces that, according to certain information reaching the French Government, German columns are flying white flags in the hope that the French troops will discontinue their resistance. The announcer says: "All combatants, French and Allied, on land, on sea and in the air, are reminded that no armistice or suspension of hostilities has supervened. Negotiations alone are contemplated, and they have not yet begun. It is the duty of all, therefore, to continue the resistance."

Premier Pétain and General Weygand issue an order in the evening that all French land, sea and air forces are to "continue resistance" at the side of Great Britain until there is assurance that Chancellor Hitler and Premier Mussolini will agree to an armistice on honorable terms. At the same time, all French cities and towns of more than 20,000 population are for practical purposes surrendered to the Germans by an official proclamation declaring them to be "open cities." This proclamation is made in the hope of saving them, like Paris, from bombardment. Minister of Interior Charles Pomaret who makes the announcement over the radio also orders all civilians to halt immediately their "immense and tragic" flight southward and to remain in their homes even if they are "on the point of being invaded." Order is the first element of a country's security, he says, and food supplies can be assured only if every civilian remains in his place. The French Minister for Refugees estimates that six millions are homeless.

In the evening, Madrid reports that the decisions taken by

Hitler and Mussolini at Munich have been transmitted to the German Embassy in Madrid, and are being passed on to the Spanish Foreign Office. They will be sent overnight to José Felix Lequerica, Spanish Ambassador to France, who is with the French Government at Bordeaux. Nothing specific is disclosed, but it is rumored that the eventual terms will be unconditional surrender, including the giving up of the French fleet.

The actual position of the French fleet remains uncertain. Several important fighting units are in any case operating with the British fleet at Alexandria, under the orders of a British admiral. Certain other naval units are said to have left French ports during the day for undisclosed destinations. The attitude of individual commanders towards an eventual order for surrender cannot be foretold. Meanwhile, the Spanish press reports that airplanes have been sighted over the Balearic Islands, flying in the direction of Africa. This suggestion that perhaps French planes are fleeing to Algeria is never confirmed. The situation in Syria and French North Africa is also obscure. Reports reaching French circles in London are that General Mittelhauser in Syria and General Auguste Noguès in French Morocco have "probably" decided to fight on. From Bordeaux come reports by American newspapermen that the spirit of French resistance is not dead, even inside the present French Cabinet. Ex-Premier Reynaud gives Mr. P. J. Philip of the *New York Times* a one-word interview: "Fidelity."

Prime Minister Churchill tells the House of Commons in the afternoon that "the French Government will be throwing away great opportunities and casting away their future if they do not continue the war in accordance with their treaty obligations, from which we have not felt able to release them." He says, nevertheless: "However matters may go in France, or with the French Government, or with another French Government, we in this island and in the British Empire will never lose our sense of comradeship with the French people." If final victory rewards Great Britain, she will share the gains with them. Freedom will be restored to all the peoples subjugated by Germany—Czechs, Poles, Norwegians, Dutch and Belgians. Mr. Churchill reminds his listeners, however, that "it is not yet certain that military resistance by France will come to an end." He refers to "the colossal military disaster which occurred when the French High Command failed to withdraw the northern armies from Belgium at the moment when they knew that the French front was decisively broken at Sedan and on the Meuse," adding that "this delay entailed the loss of fifteen or sixteen French divisions and threw out of action the whole of the British Expeditionary Force." Mr. Churchill says that today Great Britain has 1,250,000 men under arms and 500,000 local defense volunteers; and that she is "now assured of the immense, continuous and increasing support in supplies and munitions of all kinds from the United States, and especially of the airplanes and pilots from the Dominions and across the oceans." "The Battle of France is over," and now "the Battle of Britain is about to begin." The Prime Minister concludes: "Let us therefore address ourselves to our duty, so bear ourselves that if the British Commonwealth and

Empire last for a thousand years, men will still say 'This was their finest hour'."

From London, General de Gaulle broadcasts in the evening an appeal to the French people not to cease resistance. He says: "The generals who for many years have commanded the French armies have formed a Government. That Government, alleging that our armies have been defeated, has opened negotiations with the enemy to put an end to the fighting. We certainly have been, and still are, submerged by the mechanical strength of the enemy, both on land and in the air. The tanks, the airplanes, the tactics of the Germans far more than their numbers were responsible for our retirement. The tanks, the airplanes, the tactics of the Germans astounded our generals to such an extent that they have been brought to the pass which they are in today. But has the last word been said? Has all hope disappeared? Is the defeat final? No. Believe me, I speak with knowledge and I tell you that France is not lost. The same methods which have brought about our defeat can quite well one day bring victory. For France is not alone. She is not alone—she is not alone. She has a vast empire behind her. She can unite with the British Empire, which holds the seas, and is continuing the struggle. She can utilize to the full, as England is doing, the vast industrial resources of the United States. . . . This war is a World War. In spite of all our mistakes, all our deficiencies, all our sufferings, there are in the universe sufficient means to enable us one day to crush our enemies. Shattered today by mechanical force, we shall be able to conquer in the future by stronger mechanical force.

The fate of the world depends on it." He concludes by inviting "all French officers and men who are on British soil, or who may arrive here with or without their arms," also French engineers and skilled workmen, to get into touch with him. "Whatever happens, the flame of French resistance must not and shall not be extinguished."

As a prelude to the "Battle of Britain," German planes launch their biggest air attack of the war late this evening. They drop explosive and incendiary bombs along the lower Thames River and in East Coast areas, killing and injuring numbers of civilians. It is revealed that last night and early this morning the Royal Air Force made what are described as the greatest raids of the war into Germany, striking at 12 German cities and bombing factories, airdromes, and railway centers in the Rhineland, the Ruhr Valley and the northwestern section of the Reich.

The two French newspapers in German-occupied Paris have begun blaming ex-Premier Reynaud for all France's misery. The *Matin,* appearing anonymously, recommends that he kill himself. Gustave Hervé's *Victoire* urges that Pétain form an authoritarian régime.

There are grounds for believing that Washington has not remained inactive with regard to the situation developing between France and Britain. Ambassador Bullitt decided (*cf.* July 13) to remain in Paris when the French Government fled to Tours. But his functions are being performed in part by Anthony J. Drexel Biddle, Jr., Ambassador to Poland, who had followed the Poles to France. Mr. Biddle was at first in

Angers, the seat of the Polish Government in exile, then went to Tours when the French Government established itself there, and has since been with it in Bordeaux. It is thought that through Ambassador Biddle and through the French Embassy in Washington the United States Government has been able to send Foreign Minister Baudouin intimations of the concern felt in American official circles over a possible surrender of the French fleet to Germany, this being a matter which affects the relative naval strength of the United States. It appears that today the French Foreign Minister has let Washington know that American apprehensions on this score are unnecessary in view of the personal assurances already given privately by various members of the French Government, himself included.

The United States House of Representatives adopts the resolution passed yesterday by the Senate against changes in title of European possessions in the Western Hemisphere. A bill is also introduced to increase the nation's naval strength by 70 percent and provide a navy adequate to defend both its coasts and all its possessions. President Roosevelt at his press conference indicates that a scheme of compulsory government service for all young men and women is being studied. In two neighboring countries plans for military conscription are making progress. The Canadian Government today introduces a bill for immediate conscription for home service of able-bodied males up to 45 years, only exempting those needed for vital industries. The Mexican Cabinet approves a compulsory military training law affecting all males between 18 and 45 years.

June 19

Yesterday Bordeaux was waiting anxiously for the German reply to Premier Pétain's request for an armistice. This morning it arrives *via* Madrid. Air raid warnings during the night have not calmed the nerves of either populace or officials. Newspapermen report the city a bedlam. At 9 A.M. the French Cabinet assembles, with President Lebrun presiding. A communiqué issued later merely reports that the German note has been transmitted by the Spanish Ambassador, and that according to its terms the Reich Government is ready to present its conditions for the cessation of hostilities. As soon as the French plenipotentiaries are named (continues the communiqué), the German Government will say where and when it will receive them. The announcement is made that they have already been appointed, but the names are not made public.

Although the French Government refuses to admit that preliminary conditions have been set by Germany, there seems reason to believe that agents of the two governments have exchanged views through the Spanish Ambassador. Reports current in Bordeaux are that the terms which Germany intends to impose are so humiliating that they cannot possibly be accepted. Indeed, it is even believed in many quarters that the Government has now reverted to the idea of moving to French North Africa and continuing the struggle from there. This rumor receives some confirmation from the fact that the Government has practically decided to move to Perpignan, a city in the extreme south of the country and close to several little

Mediterranean ports which give easy access to French Morocco and Algeria. Also, it is well known that certain deputies and former cabinet ministers still are urging that the war be continued outside of France proper, on the theory that Germany's treatment of France will not thereby be made any the worse; that the Pétain-Weygand tendency to believe Britain already beaten may be incorrect; and that all help should be given toward a British victory as the only hopeful way out of France's desperate plight. Some two dozen deputies who are said to hold this view, including MM. Daladier, Mandel, Delbos and Campinchi, have today boarded the steamship *Massilia* at Le Verdon, on the Gironde estuary, with French North Africa as their destination. (Later on, they will be severely criticized by government spokesmen on this account, indeed some of them who are army officers as well as deputies will be accused of desertion. At Vichy on July 10, however, M. Herriot will compel M. Laval to acknowledge that the French authorities have facilitated the departure of the *Massilia*. Some will interpret this as indicating that at the present juncture the Pétain Government really had an intention of joining the "die hards" in French North Africa; others that members of the Government merely were willing to see their political rivals lay themselves open to the charge of being cowards and deserters.) By afternoon the idea of moving to Perpignan is more or less abandoned. It is not till late in the evening, however, that the French Government sends to Madrid the names of the four French plenipotentiaries for transmission to Berlin. Some observers attribute the delay to the difficulty of finding a formula which Germany will accept for camouflaging the surrender of the French fleet. Whether or not the Germans will occupy all of France supposedly depends on the disposal of the French fleet.

Several high British officials have reached Bordeaux to argue against any French tendency to turn the French fleet over to Germany. They include the First Lord of the Admiralty, Mr. A. V. Alexander; the First Sea Lord, Sir Dudley Pound; and Lord Lloyd, Colonial Minister. They have conversations with Premier Pétain, Foreign Minister Baudouin and other French statesmen. They renew earlier offers of British warships and other vesesls to help transport French troops and officials to North Africa should the Government decide to prolong resistance. (They subsequently will maintain that in these talks they received many assurances that France would fulfill her undertaking under the Anglo-French Agreement of March 28. But it will not be claimed in London that the British Ambassador in Bordeaux ever was able to secure a formal assurance regarding the French fleet from the Pétain Government, though the matter was brought formally to its attention by Prime Minister Churchill the same evening it took office.) Mr. Alexander leaves for home from the Biscarosse airport soon after midnight.

In London, meanwhile, every item of news from Bordeaux is being closely scanned and the claim is made that some slight but encouraging change can be noted in the attitude of the Pétain Government. The Diplomatic Correspondent of the *Times* finds that the French Government is laying greater emphasis on its determination to fight rather than accept terms

which are dishonorable; also that it seems to be giving more
encouragement to the French armies which still are carrying
on courageous rearguard actions. Before each announcement
on the French radio still come the slow, distant-sounding notes
of the Marseillaise—"Aux armes, citoyens!" The announcements themselves are shorter and sound more resolute. "Let us
wait calmly," says one broadcast heard in London, "and let us
have full confidence in the men who in a most tragic hour have
taken on the heavy burden of responsibility for the country's
destiny. Let us thank all our soldiers who are fighting unceas-
ingly with fierce energy and with a courage more than human."
The director of the French radio services, in a broadcast explaining the request for an armistice, says that while the Government is ready to put an end to the struggle, it will "not
accept anything that interferes with the structure of our country. We are capitulating with honor, but if it is sought to impose upon France conditions incompatible with that honor she
will continue the struggle with her Allies." On the other hand,
Minister of the Interior Pomaret has publicly rebuked General
Charles de Gaulle for having urged in his broadcast from London last evening that resistance against Germany be kept up.
M. Pomaret says General de Gaulle has been ordered back to
France.

The retreat of the French forces continues. The Germans
push ahead relentlessly in western and central France, while
in Burgundy motorized troops are already in Lyon, only 200
miles from the Mediterranean. The French are still resisting in
the Maginot Line on both sides of Thionville; but the Germans

claim the capture of Lunéville and Toul and say Strasbourg has been entered and the swastika raised. Almost half of France is in German hands.

Germany makes it clear that Italy will have no part in the meeting between the French and German representatives. A Berlin spokesman explains that "Italian interests are in good hands after yesterday's Munich agreement." Berlin stresses that nothing less than the complete capitulation of France will satisfy Chancellor Hitler. The *Völkischer Beobachter* comments that Germans are not revengeful, but "have at last ceased to be good-natured German blockheads." The *Berliner 12 Uhr Blatt* writes: "The old Europe was the product of the blind and furious hatred of a Richelieu and a Clemenceau. The new Europe will be built by the love and faith of the Fuehrer."

Reports reaching London indicate that Europe faces a major famine this coming winter. Germany's food situation is described as bad, but things are even worse in the occupied countries, as the Germans have been removing livestock, fodder and reserves of provisions.

The note of the United States of June 17 to Germany and Italy warning those Powers to keep their hands off the Western Hemisphere is released to the press. The Government's position is reinforced by an announcement by Under Secretary of State Welles that two days ago the United States also delivered invitations to the other American Republics to meet for a discussion of the new problems in the Western Hemisphere arising from the European conflict. Mr. Welles says that 16 nations have already replied favorably.

Lord Lothian, British Ambassador, tells 1,200 alumni of Yale University that "if Hitler beats us, the totalitarian Powers will possess airplane building facilities, naval and shipbuilding dockyards and industrial resources all over Europe, and especially in Germany, France and Britain, to say nothing of Italy, which will enable them vastly to outbuild your own defensive preparations, whatever they may be, and that indefinitely." He adds that "if Hitler gets our fleet, or destroys it, the whole foundation on which the security of both our countries has rested for 120 years will have disappeared."

Japan announces that she considers maintenance of the *status quo* in French Indo-China "equally important" to its maintenance in the Netherland Indies. A Foreign Office spokesman informs the press that Japan's interest in Indo-China arises from her position as the "stabilizing" influence in the Far East, and also from concern over the munitions traffic through the French colony. The Japanese Government is understood to have informed Germany and Italy that it expects to be consulted concerning the future of Indo-China, on the grounds that Japan's interests there are both military and economic.

Chapter VIII

THE ARMISTICE WITH GERMANY
AND ITALY

June 20

THE MESSAGE from the Pétain Government announcing the names of its four plenipotentiaries, dispatched last evening by way of Madrid, is delayed in transmission and does not reach Berlin until 1 A.M. No action on it is taken until 4 A.M., when it reaches Chancellor Hitler at his army headquarters. But another type of German action occurs meanwhile, calculated to spur on the Bordeaux Government to prompt surrender. At about the moment when the French note arrives in Berlin waves of German bombers appear over the city of Bordeaux and the docks along the Gironde River. Their bombs fall over a 50–mile radius. Some of the Nazi planes sweep over the city only 400 yards above the rooftops, bombing buildings jammed with refugees and the squares where they are encamped. In the two visitations, one at 1 A.M., the other at 6 A.M., about 150 persons are killed and 300 injured. The Government had declared Bordeaux an open city, therefore not a military objective in the French view. In Rome it is announced that Italian planes aided the German air force in the attack.

On receipt of the Pétain note Chancellor Hitler gives instructions as to where and how the French representatives shall
present themselves to receive his terms. In accordance with his
orders, the French delegation, headed by General Charles
Huntziger, and including Rear-Admiral Maurice Leluc, General of the Air Force Bergeret, and Léon Noel, formerly Ambassador to Poland, leave Bordeaux later in the morning. One
story is that they use a white airplane. The United Press will
report from Bordeaux tomorrow that in fact they drive north
by motor, and are greatly delayed when they encounter retreating French troops south of the Loire. They reach the German
pontoon bridge across the Loire at Tours about midnight,
where they are met by a German officer who had been waiting
for them for some hours. They proceed to Paris and there
spend the remainder of the night. Their ultimate destination
is not disclosed in Bordeaux. But in Berlin it is said their meeting with the German delegates will take place in the historic
forest of Compiègne, where was signed in November 1918 the
armistice that ended hostilities in the First World War.

A communiqué in Rome announces: "The French Government this morning sent word to the Italian Government
through the Spanish Government asking to negotiate an armistice with Italy. The Italian Government has replied through
the same medium in terms analogous to those of the German
Government: namely, that it awaits knowledge of the names
of the French plenipotentiaries, to whom the place and date
of the meeting will later be given." While waiting for the
French reply, the Italian press, like the German, is demanding

unconditional surrender and warning against any feeling of
pity for the French. Thus the *Tevere* writes: "Stop crying for
France. What more could they have done to merit our heel in
their necks? Let that country of carrion burn once and for all
in the torture of the direst defeat. . . . Let them stay on their
knees for centuries."

A meeting of the French Cabinet is followed by an important radio address by Marshal Pétain. He speaks as follows:

"I have asked the enemy to put an end to hostilities. The
Government yesterday appointed plenipotentiaries to receive
their conditions. I took this decision with the stout heart of a
soldier because the military situation imposed it. We had
hoped to resist on the Somme-Aisne line. General Weygand
had regrouped our forces and his name alone presaged victory. The line yielded, however, under the pressure of the
enemy, and forced our troops to retreat. From June 13 the
request for an armistice was inevitable. The blow surprised
you, and remembering 1914–1918, you sought the reasons for
it. I am going to give you them.

"On May 1, 1917, we still had 3,280,000 men under arms,
in spite of three years of murderous fighting. On the eve of
the present battle we had 500,000 fewer. In May 1918 we
had 85 British divisions; in May 1940 we only had 10. In
1918 we had with us 58 Italian divisions and 42 American
divisions. The inferiority of our matériel was even greater
than that of our effectives. French aviation has fought at
odds of one to six. Not so strong as 22 years ago, we had also

fewer friends, too few children, too few arms, too few allies. There is the cause of our defeat.

"The French people do not deny the blow. All peoples have known ups and downs. It is by the way they react that they show themselves to be weak or great. We shall learn a lesson from the battle which has been lost. Since the victory, the spirit of pleasure prevailed over the spirit of sacrifice. People have demanded more than they have given. They have wanted to spare themselves effort. Today misfortunes come. I was with you in the glorious days. As head of the Government I shall remain with you in the dark days. Stand by me. The fight still goes on. It is for France, the soil of her sons."

This address must come as a special blow to those French units which have up to the last moment been carrying on courageously against the advancing German flood. It is taken by the French public as sealing the nation's surrender even though the armistice terms are not yet known. The old Marshal probably has more prestige than any other French leader today. Even so, opinion remains divided both in France and among Frenchmen abroad about the inevitability of his decision to ask for an armistice rather than to attempt continuing resistance in company with Britain. Foreign journalists in Bordeaux report that the speech has finally awakened the city to the full extent of the national tragedy, which hitherto, somehow, has not seemed real. Marshal Pétain himself, passing today in his automobile through the streets, is the object of respectful sympathy; but there is none of the cheering which marked his appearance on previous days.

In spite of the fatalistic tone of the Pétain speech rumors again revive in Bordeaux that the French Government is preparing to leave for a new provisional capital, perhaps Biarritz. A Reuters dispatch states that the Government made a decision in this sense after the bombing attack of this morning in order to remove all excuse for the Germans to consider Bordeaux anything but an open town. There continues to be great confusion as to the status of what are called the "negotiations" with Germany. The United Press says that the French emissaries, having crossed the Nazi lines, already have received Hitler's conditions. It revives the report that if these prove too strong the Government may go to North Africa. The Rome radio announces that the French representatives have already returned to Bordeaux. None of these reports coincides with actual developments.

At a late hour in the evening Berlin still has not announced the names of the German delegates to tomorrow's meeting. Officials continue to be uncommunicative about the terms to be imposed, but comments by the Nazi press leave no doubt that Germany will claim overflowing vengeance for what took place in 1918. The *Nachtausgabe* says that the French delegates will receive an ultimatum of unconditional surrender, involving the complete and permanent military annihilation of France. It writes: "The hour of pity in Europe is past." Though the press refrains from speculating about specific terms, it universally assumes that French territory will now serve as a German military base in the campaign against Britain. This implies at least the occupation of the French

coasts on the Channel and the Atlantic, leaving Mediterranean
areas and ports to the domination of Italy.

No armistice having yet been declared, the German armies
continue their advance. The French radio admits the fall
of Lyon, second city of France. A Nazi spearhead is driving
up the Rhône Valley towards Geneva. The Germans announce
the capture of Brest, the French naval base at the tip of Brittany, and say that further south the lower Loire from Nantes
to Tours has been crossed at many points. At Tours there
has been bitter fighting, with hand-to-hand actions being
waged in the streets of the city for many hours. Below the
Loire the Nazi bombers without respite attack the French
forces that are streaming southwards, also the refugees,
whether still on the roads or gathered in hamlets or towns.
In northern Lorraine remnants of the defeated French eastern
army are either taken prisoner or are driven still closer together in the Moselle area between Epinal and Toul and in
the central part of the upper Vosges. The German News
Agency reports that French troops in the Maginot Line north
of Metz are still resisting fiercely, though without any prospect
of relief. Berlin claims that over 200,000 prisoners were taken
yesterday alone, including General Altmeyer, commander of
the French Tenth Army.

The British Parliament meets in secret session to hold an
inquest on past military strategy and presumably to discuss
the defense problems rendered so acute by the French surrender. There is a movement afoot, especially in Labor circles, to force out Mr. Chamberlain, who still retains a place

in the Cabinet as Lord President of the Council. German planes raid England. British aircraft bomb northwest Germany, parts of occupied France and the Netherlands. The first contingents of Australian and New Zealand troops land in Great Britain. Their 10,000-mile trip has been made without an attack.

Thousands of persons whose past activities make them especially obnoxious to the present régimes of Germany and Italy, or who might find themselves in difficulties under a pro-Fascist régime in France, are seeking to leave the country. Many are trying to get to Spain or Portugal. The consulates of both countries are besieged for visas. Conditions on the Spanish frontier are chaotic. Among those admitted are the former Empress Zita of Austria-Hungary and her son, the Archduke Otto, also the three children of King Leopold of Belgium. Other refugees are making their way to England on cargo boats or on British warships. One ship arriving in Falmouth today from Bordeaux brings 1,300 refugees, among them prominent French politicians and publicists, as well as most of the English journalists who have been serving in France during the war. This and the other ships arriving during the next few days, though crowded mainly with returning British subjects and French anti-Fascists, also carry refugee German and Italian intellectuals and some contingents of the Polish and Czech forces that have been fighting in France. The Polish Embassy in London announces today that Premier Wladislas Sikorski and Foreign Minister August Zaleski have reached England safely. Members of the Belgian

Government, which has been installed in France, also are expected. Representatives of Ethiopia, Czecho-Slovakia, Norway, and the Netherlands are in London already.

The *Massilia,* carrying some two dozen French deputies, among them M. Daladier and a number of other ex-cabinet ministers, sails today from Le Verdon near Bordeaux (*cf.* June 19). It had been delayed by a strike of the crew; but the naval authorities intervened and arranged for a naval crew to man the ship for its trip to North Africa. Conflicting rumors will be flying around during the next week or so as to the vessel's whereabouts. Actually it will arrive two or three days hence in Casablanca, a seaport on the Atlantic coast of French Morocco. (About June 25 General Gort and Mr. Duff Cooper, Minister of Information, will arrive *via* Tangier at Rabat, the capital of French Morocco. They will find General Noguès, French Resident General and Commander in Chief, absent in Algiers. But his Secretary General, M. Morize, has received instructions not to permit the British envoys to communicate with ex-Premier Daladier, M. Mandel, or any of the other Frenchmen aboard the *Massilia.* General Gort and Mr. Duff Cooper will therefore leave without being able to present their argument that the French statesmen in question should continue resistance to Germany outside France proper. They will return to London by air, *via* Gibraltar, on June 27. Eventually the passengers on the *Massilia* will be brought back to France, some of them to face trial at Riom. According to statements by MM. Herriot and Jeanneney before the National Assembly at Vichy, July

10, apparently not disputed by M. Laval, they wished to return in time to attend that session, but the German-French Armistice Commission at Wiesbaden denied them transport facilities.)

The French Government has been receiving from Algeria and Tunisia, and from colonies of French citizens in various foreign countries, offers to place all their resources at its disposal if it desires to continue the war. But the eventual attitude of French military commanders in the colonies towards an armistice with Germany and Italy still remains obscure (*cf.* June 22, 23 and 24).

"Competent quarters" in Istanbul state that Turkey will never permit the installation of a Power other than France in Syria. If any change is to be made, she will accept only an independent status for Syria.

President Roosevelt nominates Henry L. Stimson as Secretary of War and Frank Knox as Secretary of the Navy, both of them Republicans. A bill for selective compulsory military service is introduced in the Senate. That body passes the $1,777,489,788 Army and Navy Emergency Appropriation Bill.

JUNE 21

Preparations for the reception of the French delegation in the Forest of Compiègne are carried out with considerable secrecy. Not until noon is it known that Chancellor Hitler himself will participate in the ceremony. He reaches the spot near Rethondes, marked by various monuments, about 3 P.M.

Awaiting him are Field Marshal Hermann Goering; Colonel General Wilhelm Keitel, Chief of Staff of the Supreme Command of the Army; Colonel General Walther von Brauchitsch, Commander-in-Chief of the Army; Grand Admiral Erich Raeder; Foreign Minister von Ribbentrop; and Rudolf Hess, Deputy Party Leader. The historic railway coach in which General Foch handed the German representatives the armistice terms on November 11, 1918, is at the original spot. Nearby is a tent, with tables and chairs for the French delegates and a large notice reminding them of the date—June 21, 1940—as though (said one newspaper writer) to expunge the previous date of 1918. Near at hand the plaque commemorating the 1918 armistice has been covered by the war standard of the German Reich, and in front of it flies Hitler's own standard. Hitler climbs into the coach. Fifteen minutes later the French delegates appear. After silently saluting the Hitler standard, they enter the car where Herr Hitler and his staff are already seated at the rectangular table. The Germans stand up and give the Nazi salute, whereupon the entire party sits down, Herr Hitler facing General Huntziger. The formalities begin. General Keitel rises and reads (in German) Hitler's introductory message, the preamble to the armistice terms and the terms themselves. Only the preamble is given to the press at this time. The actual terms, it is stated, will not be published until after they have been accepted.

The preamble begins by giving the Nazi version of what happened in 1918. The German forces laid down their arms, it says, relying on the promises of President Wilson. This ended "a war which the German people and their Government had not desired, and in which, in spite of tremendously superior forces, the enemy had not defeated the German Army, Navy or Air Force in any decisive action." Then had begun a long period of suffering, dishonor and humiliation for the German people. "On September 3, 1939,—twenty-five years after the outbreak of the World War—Great Britain and France without any reason again declared war on Germany. Now arms have decided and France is defeated. The French Government have requested the Reich Government to state the conditions for an armistice. The historic Compiègne Forest was chosen for the presentation of these conditions in order to blot out once and for all by this act of justice and restitution a remembrance which represented for France no glorious deed and which the German people felt to be the greatest humiliation of all time. France, after heroic resistance, has been defeated and has collapsed after a unique series of terrible battles. Germany does not, therefore, propose to give to the terms or negotations for an armistice the character of insult to so brave an opponent." The preamble concludes by outlining the objects of the German demands: "(1) To prevent a resumption of hostilities. (2) To provide all necessary safeguards to Germany for the continuation of the war forced upon her by Great Britain. (3) To create the necessary conditions for a new peace, the basic elements of which shall be reparation of the injustice committed by force against the Reich."

After the preamble has been read, Hitler at 3:42 P.M.

leaves the railway carriage, followed by Marshal Goering and Foreign Minister Ribbentrop. The four French delegates remain in the coach with General Keitel while a translation of the preamble and the terms is read to them by Herr Schmidt, the interpreter. Some ten minutes later they withdraw to their tent to begin a discussion of the terms. During these discussions they are in direct telephonic communication with Bordeaux. Shortly after 6 P.M. they return to the railway car to resume contact with General Keitel. The conversations continue intermittently through the evening. Late in the night the French delegates return to Paris.

Having wiped out Germany's "deepest shame of all time," Chancellor Hitler orders all traces of the 1918 humiliation removed from Compiègne. The historic railway car and memorial stone monument "to Gallic triumph" are to be shipped to Berlin. Furthermore, at the Fuehrer's orders, the positions and stones of both "armistice coach" and Kaiser Wilhelm's train will be destroyed. Only the monument to Marshal Foch is to be preserved unharmed.

Bordeaux recognizes that French military operations have ceased. The fiction of a military conference for the press is abandoned this afternoon. Isolated French armies may continue to resist for honor's sake until surrounded or annihilated, but that is all. War news now consists mainly of a record of the enemy's daily advance. Everybody is awaiting the "fatal news"—the conditions imposed by Germany. Foreign correspondents report that some people realize that the terms will be severe, but that the mass of the people know nothing and are told nothing. The papers print nothing beyond the fact that the French envoys have left for the German lines. The *Temps* speaks bluntly of the coming "Diktat." But the man in the street speaks of "peace negotiations," estimating how much French territory will have to be ceded and preparing to return home as soon as possible. The masses have failed to understand the real nature of an armistice, for the censor up to now has not permitted any discussion on this point. Today for the first time the public is informed that a request for the cessation of hostilities is an admission that it is impossible to continue the war, *e.g.,* there will be an unconditional surrender, and the conditions will be imposed by the victors. The *Petite Gironde* points out the need for making this clear in order that "when the truth can no longer be concealed" there will be "no brutal reactions" among the people.

An informal meeting of the members of the French Parliament now in Bordeaux is attended by some 50 senators and deputies. They are reported to have decided to stand by Marshal Pétain regardless of their individual opinions; and they applaud M. Laval's statement that it is not by leaving France that they can save her.

While their government's representatives discuss armistice terms the French soldiers continue to fight. A French communiqué states that the troops in the Vosges have formed themselves into a vast square and are giving battle vigorously. Berlin's evening news (according to the British United Press) is that the most bitter fighting is now taking place near Thionville, in northern Lorraine, near the Luxembourg frontier,

where the French occupy positions which are extremely difficult to capture. In general, no major advances are claimed
in western or central France, where positions reached yesterday by advance motorized units apparently are being consolidated. German bombers have been active against shipping, however, especially off La Rochelle and in the Gironde;
and the interchange of air attacks on Germany and Britain
continues.

The first that the French public hears of the British offer
of June 16 to establish an Anglo-French union is a public
announcement in Bordeaux this evening that the plan had to
be rejected because of lack of time for putting it into operation. There has been no mention of the French fleet in any of
the press dispatches from Compiègne or Berlin, nor is anything said about it at Bordeaux. But a dispatch to the *New
York Times* from Rome notes that in the Italian capital this
question is considered "the key problem of the parleys under
way."

In the evening the final text of the German terms for an
armistice reach Bordeaux from Compiègne. At 9:30 P.M.
the French radio merely announces that no precise indications can be given "concerning the actual stage of the negotiations." Word is sent to Cabinet members that they are to
meet in emergency session at 1 A.M.

Italy, meanwhile, awaits notification from France of the
names of the plenipotentiaries who will discuss armistice
terms with her direct. Rome looks on the French situation
as already liquidated. Moreover, as the British will now be

deprived of the aid of the French fleet and air force, as well as the French bases in Tunis, Corsica and Syria, they will be obliged to withdraw from the Mediterranean. Italy thus will be able to achieve all her aims. The Rome radio says in the evening that if France agrees to the German armistice terms, Italy will cöoperate with Germany in the military occupation of France.

The Associated Press reports from Cairo that the French forces and fleet in the Eastern Mediterranean seem ready to continue the war "whatever the outcome of the French-German negotiations."

Rumania, apparently feeling that she can no longer rely on Allied protection, moves towards a rapprochement with Germany. After several conferences with the German Minister, King Carol issues a decree in the evening transforming Rumania into a totalitarian state.

President Roosevelt proclaims the intention of the United States to safeguard the welfare and security of the countries of the Western Hemisphere by economic as well as military means, and invites other nations to join in the fight against totalitarian economics. He suggests an export corporation to implement the plan, with a capital of between one and two billion dollars.

JUNE 22

Shortly before midnight last night the French Cabinet was summoned to meet at 1 A.M. this morning to study the German armistice terms as transmitted by General Huntziger from Compiègne. The session lasts until 3 A.M. Individual members are up all night continuing their discussions. The Cabinet meets again after breakfast and continues in session, with brief intervals for meals, throughout the day. The wording of the preamble and its publication in advance of the detailed terms are recognized in Bordeaux as clever German manœuvers. Correspondents report that the tribute paid in the preamble to French valor and bravery has been seized on by the man in the street as helping to save French honor. The statement that Germany is to receive safeguards for prosecuting the war against England, which the British Government emphasizes would be contrary to the French pledge against a separate peace is glossed over.

After a night in Paris the French delegates return to Compiègne, reaching there at 10 A.M., and continue their deliberations throughout the day. They have direct telephone communication with Bordeaux, but the connection is bad. The French Government proposes various amendments to the original German terms; it is understood that these are accepted in some relatively unimportant cases, but most are rejected. At 6:30 P.M. General Keitel presents a written demand for a final answer within an hour. General Huntziger has trouble explaining this over the telephone to Bordeaux and in getting his Government's final assent. *The armistice is signed at 6:50 p.m.* General Keitel signs for Germany and General Huntziger for France. A little more than 27 hours have elapsed since the German demands were presented in Hitler's presence. The German account records that General Huntziger, in a choked voice, announces that his Government has ordered him to sign. "Before carrying out my

Government's order," he says, "the French delegation deems it necessary to declare that in a moment when France is compelled by fate of arms to give up the fight, she has a right to expect that the coming negotiations will be dominated by a spirit that will give two great neighboring nations a chance to live and work once more. As a soldier you will understand the onerous moment that has now come for me to sign." After the signatures are affixed, General Keitel requests all present to rise from their seats, and then says: "It is honorable for the victor to do honor to the vanquished. We have risen in commemoration of those who gave their blood to their countries."

It is announced that no details of the armistice terms will be made public until after the agreement has been reached with Italy. There is no positive assurance that the terms will be published even then. Nor does the agreement signed at Compiègne provide for immediate cessation of hostilities. It merely is stated that the fighting is to end six hours after the Italian Government has notified the German High Command of the signing of an armistice treaty between Italy and France. To execute this second treaty the French emissaries leave at once for Rome.

The Franco-German armistice provides as follows: [1]

"*Article 1:* The French Government directs a cessation of fighting against the German Reich in France as well as in French possessions, colonies, protectorate territories and mandates, as well as

[1] Based on the Associated Press translation of the official German text given out in Berlin on June 25.

on the seas. It directs the immediate laying down of arms of French units already encircled by German troops."

Article 2 provides that French territory north and west of the line shown on the map on page 145 will be occupied by German troops. Those areas which are to be occupied and which are not yet in control of German troops shall be turned over to them immediately.

"*Article 3:* In the occupied parts of France the German Reich exercises all rights of an occupying Power. The French Government obligates itself to support with every means the regulations resulting from the exercise of these rights and to carry them out with the aid of the French administration. . . . It is the intention of the German Government to limit the occupation of the west coast, after ending hostilities with England, to the extent absolutely necessary. The French Government is permitted to select the seat of its government in unoccupied territory, or, if it wishes, to move to Paris. In this case, the German Government guarantees the French Government and its central authorities every necessary alleviation so that they will be in a position to conduct the administration of unoccupied territory from Paris."

"*Article 4:* French armed forces on land, on the sea and in the air are to be demobilized and disarmed in a period still to be set. Expected are only those units which are necessary for maintenance of domestic order. Germany and Italy will fix their strength. The French armed forces in the territory to be occupied by Germany are to be hastily withdrawn into territory not to be occupied and be discharged. These troops, before marching out, shall lay down their weapons and equipment at the places where they are stations at the time this treaty becomes effective. They are responsible for orderly delivery to German troops."

Article 5 provides that Germany may demand the surrender, in good condition, of all guns, tanks, planes, means of conveyance and ammunition of French units which are still resisting and which at the time this agreement becomes effective are in the territory not to be occupied.

Article 6 provides that such of the above war materials as are not allocated to French use are to be stored under German or Italian control. The manufacture of new war material in the unoccupied territory is to be stopped immediately.

Article 7 provides that land and coastal fortifications in the occupied territory are to be surrendered to the Germans undamaged, together with the plans of these fortifications.

"Article 8: The French war fleet is to collect in ports to be designated more particularly, and under German and (or) Italian control, there to be demobilized and laid up—with the exception of those units released to the French Government for protection of French interests in its colonial empire. The peacetime stations of ships should control the designation of ports.

"The German Government solemnly declares to the French Government that it does not intend to use the French war fleet which is in harbors under German control for its purposes in war, with the exception of units necessary for the purposes of guarding the coast and sweeping mines. It further solemnly and expressly declares that it does not intend to bring up any demands respecting the French war fleet at the conclusion of a peace.

"All warships outside France are to be recalled to France, with the exception of that portion of the French war fleet which shall be designated to represent French interests in the colonial empire."

Article 9 provides that the Germans are to be given the exact location of all mines, and that they may require that French forces sweep them away.

"Article 10: The French Government is obligated to forbid any portion of its remaining armed forces to undertake hostilities against Germany in any manner.

"The French Government also will prevent members of its

armed forces from leaving the country and prevent armaments of any sort, including ships, planes, etc., being taken to England or any other place abroad.

"The French Government will forbid French citizens to fight

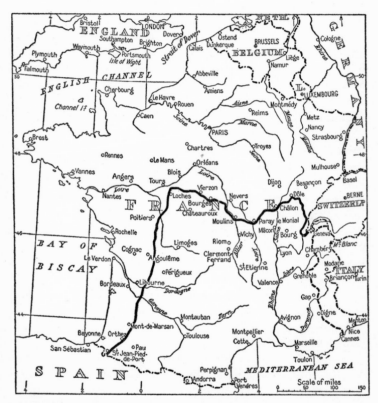

The heavy solid line on the above map shows the limits of the German zone of occupation in France, as indicated in Article 2 of the German-French Armistice of June 22. The broken line shows the approximate limits of the demilitarized zone along the Franco-Italian frontier, as specified in Article 3 of the Italian-French Armistice of June 24.

against Germany in the service of States with which the German Reich is still at war. French citizens who violate this provision are to be treated by German troops as insurgents."

Article 11 provides that no French merchant shipping may leave port until further notice without the approval of the German and Italian Governments. French merchant vessels will either be re-called by the French Government or instructed to enter neutral ports.

Article 12 provides that no airplane flights may be made over French territory without German approval. Airfields in the un-occupied territory shall be placed under German and Italian control.

Article 13 obligates the French Government to turn over to Ger-man troops in the occupied region all facilities and properties of the French armed forces, in undamaged condition; also harbors, industrial facilities and docks; also transportation and communica-tions facilities. Further, the French Government shall perform all necessary labor to restore these facilities, and will see to it that the necessary technical personnel and rolling stock of the railways be retained in service, also other transportation equipment, to a degree normal in peacetime.

Article 14 prohibits further transmission from all French wire-less stations. Resumption of wireless communication from unoc-cupied France will require special permission.

Article 15 obligates the French Government to convey transit freight between the German Reich and Italy through unoccupied territory.

"*Article 16:* The French Government, in agreement with the responsible German officials, will carry out the return of the popu-lation into occupied territory."

Article 17 obligates the French Government to prevent transfers of economic valuables and provisions from the occupied to the non-occupied territory or abroad without German permission. "In that connection, the German Government will consider the necessities of life of the population in unoccupied territory."

"*Article 18:* The French Government will bear the costs of maintenance of German occupation troops on French soil."

"*Article 19:* All German war and civil prisoners in French custody, including those under arrest and convicted, who were seized and sentenced because of acts in favor of the Reich, shall be surrendered immediately to the German troops. The French Government is obliged to surrender upon demand all Germans designated by the German Government in France, as well as in the French possessions, colonies, protectorate territories and mandates. . . ."

"*Article 20:* French troops in German prison camps will remain prisoners of war until conclusion of a peace."

Article 21 makes the French Government responsible for the security of all objects whose surrender is demanded in this agreement, and binds it to make compensation for any damage or removal contrary to the agreement.

Article 22 gives the Armistice Commission, acting in accordance with the direction of the German High Command, authority to regulate and supervise the carrying out of the armistice agreement. The French Government will send a delegation to the seat of the German Armistice Commission to present French wishes and to receive rulings with regard to them.

Article 23 provides that this agreement becomes effective as soon as the French Government has also reached an agreement with the Italian Government. Hostilities will cease six hours after the Italian Government has notified the German Government of conclusion of such an agreement.

"*Article 24:* This agreement is valid until conclusion of a peace treaty. The German Government may terminate this agreement at any time with immediate effect if the French Government fails to fulfill the obligations it assumes under the agreement."

The German High Command announces that approximately 500,000 French troops surrounded in Alsace Lorraine "have capitulated after a desperate resistance." Among them, in addition to many other high officers, are the Commanders of the Third, Fifth and Eighth Armies. A later communiqué says that only isolated sections of the Maginot Line in Lower Alsace and Lorraine, and certain units in the Vosges, continue to resist. In Brittany, the important harbor towns of St. Malo and Lorient have been occupied. Berlin puts the number of prisoners taken in western France in the past few days at over 200,000.

The French High Command reports that during the day German units pushed south of the lower Loire, and that the German thrust down the Rhône toward the junction with the Isère is somewhat intensified. On the southern front, the Italians have attacked at several points from Mont Blanc to the sea, but according to the French High Command they have been held. According to Swiss reports, a body of men belonging to the French Foreign Legion, their backs to the Swiss frontier and completely cut off from other French troops, have repulsed Nazi assaults against the forts of L'Ecluse and Le Joux. The town of Bellegarde near Fort L'Ecluse is lost to the Germans, regained, and then lost again between dawn and dusk. Bitter fighting is said to continue in this section.

General de Gaulle in an evening broadcast from London repeats his request of June 18 for the support of "all French people who wish to remain free." He says that an armistice will be not only a capitulation but "a submission to slavery."

The French people have lost the Battle of France, but "there remains to us a vast empire, an intact fleet, much gold; and honor, common sense, and the interest of the country demand that all free Frenchmen should fight wherever they are."

The French colony at Beirut telegraphs to President Lebrun and Marshal Pétain stating that it puts all its confidence in them for safeguarding French honor, and placing at their disposal all its resources, material and moral. It implores the French leaders "to make every effort to continue the struggle, in company with our Allies and with the Anglo-French fleet, in the territories of the French Empire, territories which the enemy has not penetrated and which intend to continue an indomitable resistance." General Mittelhauser, French commander in Syria, telegraphs to the French colony in Egypt thanking it for its message of June 20 to President Lebrun and stating that "Frenchmen overseas with their forces still intact, constitute a sure token of victory. The French Army and residents in the Levant are at one with you." (*Cf.* June 20 and 24.)

Three hours after the signature of the armistice at Compiègne the fact is notified to the German people by radio, though the actual terms are withheld. Later a transcription of General Huntziger's words is also put on the air. The *Angriff* predicts: "After this war France will take the first step toward a new era which the young authoritarian states of Europe have already taken."

Late in the evening the French Government announces officially the signature of the armistice with Germany, on "hard but honorable" terms. The terms are not given out. (Even after some months it will remain doubtful whether they have ever been published in full in France.)

Fascist quarters in Rome believe that French possessions in Africa will be demilitarized in a few days under the terms of the Italian-French armistice, leaving Italy's armed forces free to deal with Britain in the Mediterranean and Africa. The semi-official *Relazioni Internazionali* writes: "Once the French problem has been solved Italian and German armies must crush the British hegemony. . . . England will be totally occupied and the British Empire will be cut into pieces. Although Italy and Germany have not issued any common declaration on the aims of their war, as the French and British did, the Axis partners have in common their revolutions, their chiefs, and they have a single ideal and a single will. This is the true foundation of their victorious success."

JUNE 23

Early this morning Prime Minister Churchill for the second time appeals to the French people over the heads of their leaders. In a statement issued in London he says that the British Government "have heard with grief and amazement that the terms dictated by the Germans have been accepted by the French Government at Bordeaux. They cannot feel that such, or similar terms, could have been submitted to by any French Government which possessed freedom, independence, and constitutional authority." Such terms, "if accepted by all Frenchmen," would place not only France but the French Empire entirely at the mercy of the German and Italian Dictators. "Not only would the French people be held down and forced to work against their ally, says Mr. Churchill, "not only would the soil of France be used with the approval of the Bordeaux Government as the means of attacking their ally, but the whole resources of the French Empire and of the French Navy would speedily pass into the hands of the adversary for the fulfilment of his purpose." The British will be able to carry on the war to a successful conclusion. "When Great Britain is victorious," he continues, "she will, in spite of the action of the Bordeaux Government, cherish the cause of the French people, and a British victory is the only possible hope for the restoration of the greatness of France and the freedom of its people." He concludes: "Brave men from other countries overrun by Nazi invasion are steadfastly fighting in the ranks of freedom. Accordingly His Majesty's Government call upon all Frenchmen outside the power of the enemy to aid them in their task and thereby render its accomplishment more sure and more swift."

Following the issuance of Mr. Churchill's statement, the British War Cabinet sits for two and a half hours to determine how best to defend the British Isles and Empire now that the French capitulation has left them fighting alone against Germany and Italy.

The Bordeaux Government meets at 11:30 A.M. with President Lebrun presiding. Pierre Laval is appointed Minister of State and Vice-Premier, and M. Adrien Marquet is appointed Minister of State. M. Laval states in an interview that out of France's misfortune some good should come. "We must and we will rebuild," he says. "France will live again."

Ex-Premier Reynaud has been offered the French Ambassadorship at Washington by the Pétain Government, and has accepted. The French Embassy there receives notification of the appointment today; but an hour or so later word arrives from Bordeaux that it has been cancelled.

The French Government strips General de Gaulle of his military rank. In an official statement, the Government says that General de Gaulle will be tried at the "earliest court martial," charged with refusing to return to his post and with addressing an appeal to French officers and soldiers while abroad.

The French newspaper *Le Temps* asserts that if Great Britain had been able to send a large and well-equipped army to France, the nation would not have been compelled to sue for peace on Chancellor Hitler's terms. In the evening the French radio announces that during the day the last of the B.E.F. have been taken back to England. No announcement is made regarding the Polish and Czech troops in France; but as many of these as possible are being transported to England in British warships, some from Brittany, others from St. Jean de Luz, others from Cette and other Mediterranean ports. The 6,000 Polish troops in Syria will cross into Palestine later this week to join the British there.

Marshal Pétain, in a broadcast this evening, says that the French Government and people heard the statement of Prime Minister Churchill "with grief and amazement." He continues: "We can understand the anguish that prompted it. Mr. Churchill fears that the fate that has fallen upon our country during the past month may overtake his own. Mr. Churchill is a good judge of the interest of his country, but not of ours, and still less of French honor. Our flag remains unstained. Our army has fought loyally. Inferior in armaments and in numbers, it had to ask for a cessation of the fighting. It did so, I affirm, in independence and in dignity. No one will succeed in dividing Frenchmen in the hour when their country is suffering."

The airplanes bringing the French delegates to Rome reach the Littorio airfield about 3 P.M. Their whereabouts have been something of a mystery. According to the Rome correspondent of the *New York Times* they drove from Compiègne to Munich last night, and this morning came on by air to the Italian capital. The delegation is the same as at Compiègne, plus General Parisot, former French Military Attaché in Rome. After a brief welcome by Italian officials the delegates drive to the Villa Manzoni, about five miles north of Rome. Some Italian officials join them there, and preliminary discussions begin. Around 7 P.M. the French delegation motors to the Villa Incisa, 12 miles from Rome, where further negotiations take place. Mussolini is not present. The Italian plenipotentiaries are Count Ciano, Foreign Minister; Marshal Pietro Badoglio, Chief of the General Staff; Admiral Domenico Cavagnari, Naval Chief of Staff; General Francesco Pricolo, Chief of the Air Staff; and General Mario Roatta, Army Corps Commander. They greet the Frenchmen with the Fascist salute. The two groups then sit down on opposite sides of a table. Count Ciano rises and announces that on Premier Mussolini's orders Marshal Badoglio will give the armistice conditions to the French plenipotentiaries. Marshal Badoglio then asks General Roatta to read them, which he does. General Huntziger says the French delegates have taken note of the terms and asks to be allowed to convey them to the French Government, "giving the decision at the next meeting." The French delegates return to the Villa Manzoni, where they spend the greater part of the night discussing the terms among themselves and by telephone with the Bordeaux Government. The terms are not disclosed; Rome is full of reports that Italy will occupy the Mediterranean coast of France or that perhaps a buffer state will be created around Nice in the corner of France adjoining Italy.

General de Gaulle, in an evening broadcast in French from London, announces the formation of a Provisional French National Committee. He begins by saying that the Bordeaux Government capitulated before all its means of resistance had been exhausted. "There is no longer on the soil of France herself any independent Government capable of upholding the interests of France and of the French overseas. Moreover our political institutions are no longer in a position to function freely, and the people of France have at the moment no opportunity of expressing their true will. Consequently, and owing to *force majeure,* a French National Committee will be formed, in agreement with the British Government, representing the interests of the country and the people and resolved to maintain the independence of France; to honor the alliances to which she is committed; and to contribute to the war efforts of the Allies until the final victory." The Committee will account for its acts either to a legal French Government as soon as one exists, or to the representatives of the people as soon as they can assemble freely. Meanwhile it will take under its jurisdiction all French citizens now on British territory.

General de Gaulle's speech goes out over the facilities of the British Broadcasting System. He is followed on the radio by a British announcer who says in French: "His Majesty's Government find that the terms of the armistice, just signed in contravention of agreements solemnly made between the Allied Governments, reduce the Bordeaux Government to a state of complete subjection to the enemy and deprive it of all liberty and all right to represent free French citizens. The Government therefore now declare that they can no longer regard the Bordeaux Government as the government of an independent country." Britain, it is declared, has decided to recognize the Provisional French National Committee, which is determined to observe the treaty obligations of France, in preference to the Bordeaux Government.

The terms of the armistice imposed upon France leave no room for hope in England that any vestige of resistance can be maintained on the Continent. There still remains the hope, however, that parts of the French Colonial Empire and units of the French fleet will continue to fight beside the British. In this connection, the following statement is issued in London in the evening: "The signature of the armistice by the French Government brings to an end the organized resistance of the French forces at home. In the French Colonial Empire, however, there are encouraging signs that a more robust spirit prevails." Reference is made to various statements or actions by General Mittelhauser in Syria; by the Governor-General of Indo-China; by the Resident-General in Tunis; and by various military or civil authorities in Morocco, Senegal, Cameroun and Jibuti. The whereabouts of the various units of the French fleet is a closely guarded secret. British officials will not discuss the matter. An Admiralty spokesman says: "There is no speculation about it even invited in this country."

A French army communiqué states that the military situation is without notable change except along the Atlantic coast, where the Germans continue their advance towards Rochefort and Cognac. On the Alpine front Italian attempts to progress are still held in check. A German communiqué states that the battle in Alsace and Lorraine ended yesterday with the capitulation of the French armies.

Edwin C. Wilson, American Minister to Uruguay, in a speech at Montevideo at a luncheon given by the Uruguayan Foreign Minister for the officers of the *U.S.S. Quincy,* says that he is "authorized to state that it is the intention and the avowed policy of my Government to coöperate fully, whenever such coöperation is desired, with all the other American Governments in crushing all activities that arise from non-American sources and that imperil our political and economic freedom."

June 24

During the morning the French delegates study the Italian conditions at the Villa Manzoni. In the afternoon they proceed again to the Villa Incisa, where the full Italian delegation awaits him. The afternoon session does not have the calm and formal character of the first meeting, and as the hours pass and high Italian officers drive back and forth between the Villa and Premier Mussolini's office in the Palazzo Venezia the impression deepens that these negotiations are less of a cut-and-dried affair than was the German-French parley. The Pétain Government cannot lose sight, however, of the fact that although they have made terms with Germany they still are formally at war with that country, and that French soldiers will continue being sacrificed until after an agreement has been signed with Italy.

Sir Ronald Campbell, British Ambassador to France, has left Bordeaux overnight aboard a British destroyer, accompanied by the remaining members of his staff. They will reach London tomorrow.

Chancellor Hitler, who is sightseeing in Paris, visits the Eiffel Tower and the tomb of Napoleon.

In London, General de Gaulle is asked who will form the proposed National Committee. He replies that this will depend on the arrival of certain important personalities reported to be *en route* from France to Britain. (However, rumors that ex-Premier Reynaud is coming to London do not materialize; nor is it true, as reported on several occasions, that ex-Premier

Blum or ex-Premier Herriot visit England. All stay in southern France and will be present at the meeting of the French Parliament at Vichy on July 9. M. Reynaud will be seriously injured in an automobile accident near Montpellier on June 28, at which time Countess de Portes is killed; and he will appear at Vichy with his head swathed in bandages.) In a statement to the Press Association General de Gaulle says he has "reason to believe that the French fleet will not surrender." He also says that he is in telegraphic communication with General Noguès, commander of the French forces in Morocco, with General Mittelhauser, French commander in Syria, and with General Catroux, in charge of French forces in Indo-China, and expresses the conviction "that all parts of the French Empire will go on fighting." (Actually, urgent messages and commands from General Weygand to Generals Mittelhauser and Noguès will suffice to hold them in line with the policy of the Bordeaux Government.)

The French Government issues an official statement in Bordeaux, through M. Prouvost, Propaganda Commissioner, criticizing Britain's "insufficient" war effort as well as her current policy towards France. The assertion is made that the French had been led to expect to see 26 British divisions in France "in the first months of the war." The statement continues: "The Daladier and Reynaud Governments continually drew to the British Government's attention our difficulty in maintaining under arms men 48 years old, while young Britishers of 28 years had not yet been mobilized." It comments that "England, as at the time of Pitt, believed in the efficacy of the blockade and the Government continued to rule England in accordance with compromises and traditions." The statement then proceeds to give the French version of what happened at the critical Cabinet meetings in Tours on June 12 and 13 (*cf.* under the second of these dates). Regarding events after France requested an armistice, it says: "The Government considered that it was its duty to remain in France and share the fate of all Frenchmen. . . . It was in complete independence that the French Government took its decision and definitely refused to go abroad. Some members of Parliament and former Ministers thought otherwise. French public opinion will have no indulgence for them. . . ." The statement asks Great Britain "to receive only with extreme caution those Frenchmen our country disavows and wants to forget at any price, and not to allow London to become a hotbed of agitation for politicians and dissenters." It concludes: "Our foreign policy will be dictated neither by England, nor by Germany and Italy. It will be purely French." British "authoritative circles" will reply tomorrow that the foregoing French statement is "inaccurate throughout." Denial will be made that the British Government ever promised to send 26 divisions to France in the early months of hostilities; quite the contrary, it was explained in the course of staff conversations that "during the first year of the war the British military effort must be on a limited scale." The statement will continue: "In the event, 400,000 British troops were sent to France, a contribution which, as Mr. Churchill explained in the House of Commons on June 18, came up to the undertaking assumed by His Majesty's Government. The British air contribution was greatly in excess of that promised and arranged with the French General Staff. It is true that owing to shortage of equipment fewer classes were called up in Great Britain than in France; but M. Prouvost takes no account of the fact that hundreds of thousands of volunteers of over 28 years of age were incorporated in the British forces."

This morning's French communiqué speaks of fighting near St. Etienne. In the Alps, Italian attacks are said not to be making any important progress. A later communiqué—the last French war communiqué to be issued—adds the information that slight progress is being made by the Germans in the Charente, where they occupy Angoulême, and in Savoie, where they reach Aix-les-Bains. In the Alps the Italian attacks continue, but are checked everywhere except in the Maurienne district, where enemy troops advance just beyond the village of Lanslebourg, a French customs station two or three miles from the frontier, and on the coast, where they enter Menton, An Italian bulletin announces that a general attack which was started on June 21 from Mont Blanc to the sea met strong enemy resistance, but that this "did not slow down the impetuous advance of our troops, who everywhere achieved notable successes." It claims that Italian troops have taken certain important fortified works near Briançon and at Razet, and that larger units have reached the bottom of the valleys of the River Isère and its small tributary, the Arc, and of two small tributaries of the River Durance. The German communiqué states that the Atlantic coast has been occupied down to the Gironde estuary.

Late in the afternoon agreement is reached in Rome between the French and Italian delegations. A French Cabinet meeting at Bordeaux accepts the proposed text. *The Italo-French armistice is signed at 7:15 p.m., General Huntziger signing for France and Marshal Badoglio for Italy.* Afterwards the following statement is broadcast by the Rome radio: "The Italian Government have notified the French Government that the signing of the Armistice Convention between Italy and France was communicated to the German Government this afternoon at 7:35 P.M., Italian summer time. As a consequence hostilities between Italy and France will cease at 1:35 A.M Italian summer time tomorrow morning, June 25, 1940, year XVIII of the Fascist Era."

At 9 P.M. the following special communiqué is issued in Berlin: "Today, Monday, June 24, at 7:15 P.M. the Treaty of Armistice was signed between Italy and France. The Reich Government were informed at 7:35. The Treaty of Armistice between Germany and France has therefore entered into force. The Commander-in-Chief of the Armed Forces has ordered the cessation of hostilities against France at 1:35 A.M on June 25. The war in the West is therefore ended." Soon afterwards loudspeakers in the streets of Berlin blare forth the news. Hitler issues a proclamation reading: "My People: Your soldiers after barely six weeks of heroic struggle against a brave opponent have ended the war in the West. Their deeds will go down to history as the most glorious victory of all time. We humbly thank the Almighty for his blessing. I order flags to be flown throughout the Reich for ten days and Church bells to be rung for seven days."

The terms of the Franco-Italian armistice are not yet announced, but they provide (according to the text to be published in Rome tomorrow evening) as follows:

"Article 1: France will cease hostilities in her metropolitan territory, in French North Africa, in the colonies, and in territories under French mandate. France will also cease hostilities in the air and on the sea."

"Article 2: When the armistice comes into force, and for the duration of the armistice, Italian troops will stand on their advanced lines in all theatres of operations."

"Article 3: In French metropolitan territory, a zone situated between the lines referred to in Article 2 and a line drawn fifty kilometers as the crow flies beyond the Italian lines proper shall be demilitarized for the duration of the armistice.[1]

"In Tunisia, the militarized zone between the present Libyan-Tunisian frontier and the line drawn on an attached map shall be demilitarized for the duration of the armistice. In Algeria and in French African territories south of Algeria that border on Libya, a zone 200 kilometers wide adjoining the Libyan frontier shall be demilitarized for the duration of the armistice. For the duration of hostilities between Italy and the British Empire and for the duration of the armistice, the French Somaliland coast shall be entirely demilitarized. Italy shall have full and constant right to use the port of Jibuti with all its equipment, together with the French section of the Jibuti-Addis Ababa railway, for all kinds of transport."

[1] No more precise definition of the line is given. So far as known, the Italian troops in 14 days of war against France took several narrow Alpine border areas between the Swiss frontier and the Mediterranean, including the town of Briançon, about five miles from the frontier, and Menton, a Mediterranean port about a mile from the frontier. No mention is made in the armistice terms of Nice, Savoy and Corsica, French territories long demanded by Fascist Italy. (*Cf.* map on p. 145.)

Article 4 provides that zones to be demilitarized shall be evacuated by French troops within ten days, except for the personnel necessary to supervise and maintain fortifications and military buildings.

Article 5 provides for the removal within 15 days of such arms and supplies in the demilitarized zones as Italy does not require France to surrender under Article 10. Fixed armaments in the coastal territory of French Somaliland are to be rendered useless.

Article 6 requires that so long as hostilities continue between Italy and Britain the maritime fortified areas and naval bases of Toulon, Bizerta, Ajaccio and Oran shall be demilitarized.

Articles 7 and 8 concern the procedure to be followed in demilitarizing the areas and bases mentioned in Article 6.

Articles 9 through 26 parallel in a general way the main provisions in Articles 4, 5, 6, 8, 10, 11, 12, 14, 15, 19, 21 and 24 of the German armistice.

Neutral diplomatic circles in Berlin hear that the original Italian demands were whittled down considerably. The rôle of Germany in this process, and her reasons for adopting that rôle, are the subject of much speculation and contradictory comment. It is understood that the original Italian demands included the occupation of the Mediterranean coast up to and including Marseille, on the model of the German occupation of France's Channel and Atlantic coasts.

Today for the first time the French people have begun to hear what the Germans are requiring of them, but only through the British radio and other round-about methods. It was Germany's desire to keep the terms secret until the last Frenchman had laid down his arms and the German armies had moved into all the promised positions. Some observers note that the limits of the occupied zone are not an improvisation but closely resemble the line which appeared on maps issued by the Nazi Party in 1938.

The French Cabinet is called to meet tomorrow at 9 A.M. to examine and ratify the final agreements between Germany, Italy and France. It is decided that tomorrow will be observed as a day of mourning, with a memorial service in the Cathedral of Bordeaux to be attended by President Lebrun and members of the Bordeaux Government. Announcement is also made officially that the Government will soon leave Bordeaux for some place outside the zone designated for German occupation. German forces will not enter the city until afterwards.

CHAPTER IX

"PEACE"

AND SO FRANCE is formally "at peace." It is 45 days since Germany loosed her attack in the Low Countries. In all, France has been at war with Germany for 9 months and 21 days; with Italy for 14 days.

The Third Republic does not long survive the catastrophe which has overwhelmed it so swiftly. But before it is transformed into an authoritarian régime it must suffer one more blow both to its material strength and to its pride. In the Commons on June 25 Prime Minister Churchill announces that the separate armistice agreement involving the surrender of the French fleet is a clear breach of the promises of the French Government. In the following days efforts are made to persuade the commanders of those French ships which are not either in English harbors or at Alexandria to take precautions so that they never can be used against Britain. The French units in question are concentrated largely in the Algerian harbor of Oran and the adjacent naval port of Mers-el-Kebir, under command of Admiral Gensoul. No satisfaction can be obtained. The British refuse to accept the thesis that Chancellor Hitler's word and the word of Signor Mussolini, as given in the armistice treaties, are adequate safeguards.

Early in the morning of July 3 a British naval officer is sent to Admiral Gensoul with a document stating that in self-defense the British cannot allow the French warships to fall into German or Italian hands, hence that the British Government makes a formal demand that the French fleet act in accordance with one of the following alternatives: sail in company with the British and continue the war; sail with reduced crews under British control to a British port. In either case Britain promises to return the ships to France at the end of hostilities, or to make compensation if they are damaged meanwhile. If neither course is acceptable, a third is offered the French fleet: sail with reduced crews to some French port in the West Indies, to be demilitarized and to remain there or to be entrusted to the United States for safekeeping till the war is over. An ultimatum is added, to the effect that if one of these courses is not accepted, and provided the French do not themselves sink their ships within six hours, the British fleet will sink them by force. After the expiration of the time limit, the British fleet (at 5:58 P.M) opens fire. The French fleet and shore batteries reply. When the action is over the French fleet has been destroyed, with the exception of a few vessels which escape to Toulon, including the battle cruiser *Strasbourg*.

Nazi anger finds expression in hyperbolic terms. The French are dazed and furious. Foreign Minister Baudouin informs Ambassador Bullitt of the British attack "in terms of the utmost indignation and strongest protest." He asks that his sentiments be transmitted to President Roosevelt, apparently in the hope that the President will act as a restraining influence on the

British in the future. On July 4 Premier Pétain decides to communicate personally with the President. His communication (unpublished) states that the French fleet received a British ultimatum "requiring them either to join the British fleet or to scuttle." The British had already moored magnetic mines to bottle up the French fleet; and when the time-limit expired they cannonaded the French ships while at anchor. He asserts that the French Government "had been lavish in its assurance that in no case could the French naval forces be utilized against Great Britain," and that to achieve this result it had stoically accepted general conditions which were exceedingly harsh. The British Government knew this. Further, "It knew that our adversaries had recognized that they could not use our fleet against England, and that the Mediterranean ports of France proper and of French North Africa were to remain free of all foreign occupation." Premier Pétain notes that he has tried hard "to reconcile the situation in which circumstances placed him" with the maintenance of "normal and friendly relations between France and Great Britain." Now what he terms "an inexcusable *coup de force*" threatens to make this impossible. He says it is his duty to establish the "responsibilities" of the situation, and that this is the object of his communication. (It will be noted that Premier Pétain apparently has not been correctly informed regarding the terms of the British ultimatum.) On July 5 the French Cabinet announces the formal breaking of diplomatic relations with Britain.

The French Government, meanwhile, has moved from Bordeaux to Clermont-Ferrand, and thence on July 2 to Vichy.

There the fact soon becomes evident that a thoroughgoing transformation is to be made in the nature of the French State. On July 9 the French Parliament votes to give the Pétain Government full powers to establish a new constitution. The vote in the Chamber of Deputies is 395 to 3; in the Senate, 225 to 1. This constitution has been drawn up mainly by Vice-Premier Laval and provides for an authoritarian government under Marshal Pétain as "Chief of State." The following day the National Assembly meets and adopts the Pétain-Laval plan (subject to a national referendum) by 569 votes to 80. Nearly one-third of the elected representatives of the French people are absent. The next day Marshal Pétain calls on President Lebrun and informs him that he has taken over his powers and added them to his own powers as Premier; and on July 12 he designates M. Laval as his eventual successor. "Liberty, Equality, Fraternity" is abolished in favor of "Work, Family, Country."

On July 14 France observes the 151st anniversary of the storming of the Bastille. Last year the national festival was the occasion for a great display of military might in the Champs Elysées, in the presence, among other notables, of Mr. Winston Churchill. This year it falls on a Sunday and is observed as a national day of mourning. From London, Mr. Churchill, now Prime Minister, broadcasts as follows:

"Who could foresee what the course of a year would bring? Who can foresee what the course of other years will bring? Faith is given to us as a help and comfort when we stand in awe before the unfurling scroll of human destiny. And I proclaim my faith that some of us will live to see a Fourteenth of July when a liberated France will once again rejoice in her greatness and in her glory, and once again stand forward as the champion of the freedom and the rights of man. When that day dawns, as dawn it will, the soul of France will turn with comprehension and kindness to those Frenchmen and Frenchwomen, wherever they may be, who in the darkest hour did not despair of the Republic."

CHAPTER X

WHY DID FRANCE FALL?

AN AMERICAN MAY, I hope, attempt to answer the question "Why did France fall?" without seeming to criticize for the sake of criticizing. France has been beaten, to the amazement of her admirers, the grief of her friends. Britain still fights, alone, indomitable. If we on this side of the Atlantic search out the reasons for the French disaster it is because we know we share in its results and because we wish in our own interest to learn the lessons if we can.

I am not a military expert and have no qualifications for passing judgment on matters of stategy. But it must be plain to anyone who has read the preceding pages that the Allies lost the war in the Low Countries and in France very quickly indeed, even more quickly than most people seem to realize.

Within a few hours of beginning their attack on Holland and Belgium the Germans had seized an essential tactical advantage. In fact, it is arguable that the armies of those two countries had already been defeated by noon on May 10. And not only was their failure to prevent the Germans from crossing the Maas and turning the defenses of the Albert Canal an almost decisive blow to Holland and Belgium; it was a strategic reverse of the first order for France and Britain. It seems to have been accentuated, moreover, by the Allied failure to realize at once its full implications. Or was the Belgian and Dutch failure hidden from the Allied High Command? That would imply both bad faith on the part of the Belgian and Dutch leadership and extreme incompetence on the part of the British and French military attachés with the two armies in question.

This first Allied reverse was followed by a catastrophe only two days later, when the German armies which had been speeding almost unhindered across the Belgian Ardennes reached and crossed the Meuse at Sedan and near Givet. Some military historians may well decide that, given the strength, equipment and disposition of the Allied troops as of May 12, and given the strength and character of the German mechanized forces which on that day were pouring through the gap on the Meuse, the Battle of France was already lost. Others will perhaps choose May 15 or 16 as the fatal date. For we now see that by then there was no longer any very substantial reason to expect that the German drive toward the Channel could be stopped.

Yet it was not General Weygand's opinion that the situation when he took over the supreme command on May 19 was desperate. He had asked for 24 hours in which to examine it. When finally he accepted the command, he told his friends that he did so with a good deal of confidence. Two days later the tip of the German spear-head reached Abbeville, isolating all the British, French and Belgian troops in the north and, in the event, condemning them to destruction, surrender or evacuation. For they were not strong and cohesive enough to cut their way south single-handed; and the French forces that General Weygand was hurriedly collecting below the Somme did not have time to prepare a concerted drive northward before the Anglo-French forces in Flanders had been paralyzed by the collapse of the Belgians. From this point of view May 23 might be taken as the finally decisive date.

The story continues at an almost equal pace. The "Weygand Line" south of the Somme was never a real line, in the sense of being an organized defensive position, and there were not enough troops to hold it in reasonable strength when, with amazing rapidity, the Germans began their second offensive on June 5. The French and a small British contingent fought there for a short time, in some cases with great stubbornness and heroism. But the French had no further reserves. Their men and matériel were inadequate to prevent the Germans from passing the river at every point seriously attacked. By June 8 the Battle of the Somme was over. The Germans pressed on to the lower Seine and turned up toward Paris. The capital was caught between their advance units and the other German forces which had meanwhile come down across the Aisne and the Ourcq to the Marne. The main industrial regions of France were by now in the hands of the enemy. Italy entered the war on June 10. The French Government had begun moving to Tours the night before. Within two days it was discussing the necessity of asking for an armistice.

How was it that all this happened so quickly? Why were

so many military critics wrong about the French Army? Why were so many friends of France wrong about the stamina of her people? The day-by-day record will have told much to anyone familiar with internal French political and social conditions. Many factors, of course, combined to bring about the country's downfall. I shall venture to set down a few. The order in which they are mentioned does not indicate their relative importance. Different observers will give them different weight.

(1) *There was a lack of coördination between French foreign policy and French military policy.*

French foreign policy after 1918 aimed generally at maintaining a certain position for France in Europe and in the world by nurturing the alliance with Great Britain and by securing her collaboration in the task of supporting the smaller European states threatened by the common enemy, Germany. France's need for allies, already plain in the first years after the World War, was accentuated by the failure to achieve a reconciliation with Germany; the failure of plans for a disarmament treaty; the rearmament of Germany, first stealthy, then open; and the steady weakening of the League machinery for collective security. In 1938 French foreign policy in the hands of M. Bonnet abandoned Czecho-Slovakia. But French pledges to Belgium and Poland were still maintained; and after the failure of appeasement had become clear in the spring of 1939 France joined Britain in offering new pledges to Rumania and Greece.

French military and foreign policy, however, did not always

evolve harmoniously. French military leaders had been the first to demand alliances with Poland, Czecho-Slovakia and other East European countries. But gradually they had been forced to come around to a less active conception of French national defense.

The turn began as early as 1923, when French public opinion compelled as patriotic a French leader as Raymond Poincaré to cut the term of military service from three years to eighteen months. He reduced it again in 1928, this time to one year. By 1930 the peace-time strength of the French Army had been reduced to 20 divisions, compared with 42 in 1914. An exception to the general trend was the lengthening of the term of service to two years in March 1935 (by a coalition government under M. Flandin), as an offset to Germany's denunciation of her disarmament obligations and her reintroduction of conscription. The reply was not sufficient. France continued to weaken progressively in relation to Germany. The process was speeded up after the failure in March 1936 to take a strong stand against Germany's remilitarization of the Rhineland. General Gamelin was ready to risk a showdown with Germany at that time; but the interim Sarraut cabinet then in office was weak (though M. Sarraut himself favored a strong stand). This outstanding opportunity to check Hitler was let slip. Partly, no doubt, as a result of French and British weakness on this occasion, Belgium in the autumn gave notice that henceforth she would follow a course of complete independence and neutrality alike towards France and England and towards Germany. This meant that the French Army could not be sure of being able to use the Belgian fortifications against Germany or of having the support of the Belgian Army. The need for a passive conception of France's military rôle further impressed the French General Staff after Munich; henceforward French strategy would have to do without the Czech troops, air force and munitions plants, without the Czech "Little Maginot Line," and without the hope that these would keep at least 30 German divisions busy in case Germany found herself at war on two fronts at once.

From this point on the French Staff felt that a war with Germany could be won only by sitting behind the Maginot Line and by gradually starving the enemy out by means of a blockade enforced by the British and French fleets. Strategic caution was intensified by the pacifist temper of the times. We may recall that after the war had actually begun, in December 1939, Premier Daladier promised that there would be no offensives and that operations would be "sparing of French blood."

The appeals for military help received from Holland and Belgium on the morning of May 10 gave fearful emphasis to the disparity between what had remained the official policy of the Quai d'Orsay and the estimates of the military situation prepared at the Invalides and the Ministry of Defense. France's honor and political interest demanded that she carry out her pledge to Belgium (she had no obligation to Holland). Yet the actual manner in which the French Army proceeded to help was unsuccessful. Whose, and what, was the fault?

Apparently the trouble was not, as some have suggested,

that no careful plans had been laid for an advance into Belgium and Holland. It rather was that the General Staff did not like the idea of such an advance and yet had never taken a decisive stand against it. The British had always favored an expedition into the Low Countries; they naturally wanted the Germans to be kept away from the Channel coasts. The French General Staff, however, had opposed the plan, *unless*: (1) careful and detailed preparations were concerted beforehand with the Belgian and Dutch General Staffs; and (2) the Belgian and Dutch Governments agreed to permit Allied troops to cross their territories to get at Germany in case the Allies found themselves at war with her and this seemed a desirable tactic. But despite the French Army's misgivings, and even though its prerequisites had not been met, it had not definitely refused to undertake the expedition. The pledge to help Belgium in case of German attack still remained part of the French program. This was the first fault.

The second fault seems to have been that, not liking the plan for an expedition into the Low Countries, but having failed to veto it as militarily too risky, the French General Staff proceeded to execute it in its most extreme form, as though to prove that doubts about the Army's enthusiasm for it were unjustified. There were, in fact, three plans. "Dispositif No. 1" was the most sweeping. It was the one adopted by General Gamelin on the morning of May 10. Under it the Allies were to send help to the Belgians on the Albert Canal, on the supposition that the Belgian defenses there could hold out singlehanded a minimum of five days, and probably more.

When the Germans crossed the Albert Canal in the first few hours of the campaign the whole situation was changed.

That the High Command did not alter its tactics accordingly was the third error. For though honor demanded that help be sent to Belgium there was no requirement as to where or how it should be given. And as regards the Netherlands, there was no requirement to give help at all. It was purely a matter of expediency. General Giraud's rapid advance beyond Antwerp is hard to explain if the Allied High Command knew, as it should have known, that the Belgians had already lost their first battles and were in a bad way, while the Dutch were being driven rapidly back and their country already had been cut almost in two. Moreover, on May 12 the Germans had broken through General Corap's defenses on the Meuse at Sedan and Givet, threatening the Allied forces in Belgium from the southeast. Yet those forces did not receive the formal order to retire until the evening of May 15.

The "contributory negligence" of the Belgian and Netherland Governments must not be forgotten. They had stubbornly resisted offers from London and Paris to concert common means of defense with the Allies. They even had refused to concert means of defense between themselves.

The Belgian Government in October 1936 decided to follow a course of independent neutrality. In place of Locarno, just repudiated by Germany, it sought a pledge of non-aggression from Herr Hitler, and received it on October 13, 1937. Herr Hitler promised to respect Belgian independence and integrity. Meanwhile, the Belgian Government had sought release from its obligations under Locarno; this doubtless was Hitler's required *quid pro quo*. But though the British and French Governments released Belgium they continued, under the so-called "Brussels Declaration," to guarantee her. Their political object in accepting this one-sided arrangement was obviously to keep King Leopold from drifting into the German camp. The military results for France and Britain were, however, very serious. The northern French frontier was left without a sure Belgian guard and would have to be defended by a French Army already heavily reduced in numbers by the one-year service law. The situation certainly should not have been allowed to continue after September 3, 1939. Here is a fourth fault. Responsibility for it belongs partly to French political leaders, partly to the French military.

(2) *There was insufficient matériel, particularly airplanes and tanks, to repel a German attempt to turn the Maginot Line through the Netherlands and Belgium.*

The weakness in French armaments usually is blamed on the Popular Front. Students of French affairs will not accept this thesis without qualification. They know that the weakness of France's armaments relative to Germany's had been increasing steadily long before the Popular Front came into power, and that no party and only insignificant sections of public opinion had favored the financial and material sacrifices necessary to maintain a military edge over Germany. They will admit that the Popular Front insisted on instituting sweeping social reforms regardless of their effect on national defense. But they also realize this was partly due to the fact that reforms had been stubbornly resisted and were long overdue, and further, that the dampening effect of the reforms on French productivity was aggravated by the persistent refusal of earlier French Governments to take account of the realities which determined monetary policy in Great Britain and the United States.

Britain abandoned gold in the fall of 1931, the United States in April 1933. The difficulties which this entailed for the French economy became more and more obvious. But the conservative ministries of Doumergue, Flandin and Laval which preceded the formation of the Popular Front Government in 1936 (following an interim cabinet under Sarraut) all stuck to the French equivalent of a "Hoover policy" of deflation. Imports were restricted. Government salaries were cut. No great scheme of public works was initiated, as in the United States; nor was there a housing scheme to make employment, as in England, or an armaments program to make it, as in Germany. Production costs remained high; French products could not maintain their place in world markets; French productivity slumped. The results were social unrest, strikes, and a flight of capital.

The Popular Front met the sit-down strikes with a program of social reform and government expenditure. It devalued the franc in the autumn, and again in the summer of 1937. The conservatives were furious. The flight of the franc was resumed. The Left spoke of a "strike by capital" and the Right talked about the "destruction of business confidence." We cannot arbitrate these class controversies here.

But this much seems plain: The fight against the depression had been too long delayed, and the bad effects of some of the measures that aimed to put the situation right are not to be blamed solely on the authors of those measures but also on the men who had been in power earlier and who had refused to take painful action in time.

On the other hand, we cannot ignore the fact that under the Popular Front costly mistakes were made in specialized fields (e.g. aircraft manufacture) by officials who lacked the necessary technical training and authority. Also, however unobjectionable the 40-hour week may have been in theory there was a conclusive argument against adopting it in 1936: German workmen were working 48 hours a week, in certain cases much more, building up a war economy with which to overwhelm France and enslave French workmen. A similar argument ought to have prevailed over the moralistic argument for the nationalization of French war industries. It still would be a mistake to blame these errors entirely on the fact that the government which committed them was Socialistic. England under Baldwin and Chamberlain had one of the longest spans of all-powerful Conservative government in her history. Yet that Conservative government allowed preparations for British national defense, especially in the air and on land, to fall far behind what proved to be safe—far behind even what its leaders at the time knew was safe.[1]

(3) *France was divided politically and socially.*

---

[1] *Cf.* Prime Minister Baldwin's speech of November 12, 1936, explaining the slowness of his rearmament policy by the fact that a faster tempo would have been unpopular and hence could not be adopted.

A friend who had been driving an ambulance in France remarked to me the other day that all the time the French were fighting the Germans they were fighting each other also. This harsh remark is partly true. A struggle between the revolution and the counter-revolution has been in progress in France, under varying forms, ever since 1789. It was going on in 1939 and 1940. It undoubtedly is going on today. The historic reasons why there are deep divisions in French social and political life cannot be described in detail here. But it is true to say that they were partly responsible for the errors mentioned above and that they created cliques in the French Army and diminished the national will to resistance.

Fifth columnists both of the Left and of the Right were busy in France before the war began and they continued their activities after it had begun. Extreme Left groups had long been seeking to break down the liberal parliamentary régime. So had extreme Right groups. They drew encouragement from the successful foreign prototypes of the sort of government they wanted to see established in France. To some the ideal was Soviet Russia, to others it was Fascist Italy and Nazi Germany. From these countries, too, some received a more material support than mere ideological inspiration. In France, as elsewhere, the Communists followed the party line dictated from Moscow. This became particularly important after the conclusion of the Hitler-Stalin Pact, for it meant that French Communists who maintained their party affiliation were at least tacit allies of France's declared enemy. Reactionary groups like the "Croix de Feu" or the more sinister

"Cagoulards" were simply the exaggerated personification of a vague but very general preference of conservatives for authoritarian methods and ideals over the liberal methods and laical ideals of the Third Republic. (Incidentally, however, many Royalists, including the Duc de Guise himself, were more loyal to France *qua* France than were the miscellaneous pro-Fascist or pro-Nazi politicians and social climbers that one encountered in Paris. Needless to say, the *Action Française* was not in this loyal group; it was devoted to the Fascists and the Nazis, which is why the Duc de Guise always repudiated it.)

The point of importance here is that after August 1939 many men of the extreme Left and the extreme Right reached out their hands to each other around the circle. There was no official or organized "anti-Republican front." But the anti-Republican groups of the Right profited from the fact that there were powerful anti-Republican forces on the Left. And *vice versa*. Of course, the employees and admirers of the Nazi, Fascist or Communist dictatorships were not nearly so numerous as the great mass of patriotic and individualistic Frenchmen. But these good people were too unimaginative and too engrossed with their own affairs to be more than mildly impatient over the manoeuvres of extremists on either wing.

Often, too, the Republic was served by mediocre or timorous politicians. Often these were engrossed, as in other countries, with personal feuds. Thiers once said: "La République est le régime qui nous divise le moins." When France faced only the Hohenzollern armies, that "least" was not too much. When France faced the Nazis in a revolutionary world, it was fatal.

(4) *France had a Maginot Line in the mind.*

A strongly negative psychology of defense had developed gradually in France as the result of various influences, some of which have already been mentioned. Among them the love of peace and the detestation of war were particularly powerful. Just as in the United States there is a powerful appeal in the cry not to send our boys to die on foreign shores, so in France there was much sentiment against the adoption of a positive foreign policy that seemed to entail definite risks. Postponement and appeasement seemed much safer.

Also of great influence was the mere fact of the existence of the costly Maginot Line. Supposedly it was impregnable. Probably it was, from the front. Its existence came to influence French opinion as much as the Channel used to influence English opinion, or as the Atlantic and Pacific Oceans have influenced opinion in the United States. Too little attention was paid to the fact that it might be turned. As one military critic wrote (but *after* the French collapse), the Maginot Line was at once a symbol and a pretext—a symbol of French invincibility, a pretext for assuming that if Germany ever declared war she could safely be left to exhaust and defeat herself.

The defense psychology was accentuated by the let-down in morale which occurred just before, during and following Munich. The loss of the Czech citadel on Germany's other flank, and the transfer of the Skoda and other Czech munitions plants to German control, doubtless awakened French military men to the need for fresh efforts to speed up rearmament. But this was not the effect that Munich had on the most powerful organs of French public opinion. Publicists who were the favorite mouthpieces of politicians like M. Flandin, M. Laval and M. Bonnet assured the public that France need not feel greatly concerned whether the smaller European states were preserved intact or whether their resources were added to Germany's. They argued (sometimes stimulated by Herr Abetz) that friendship with Germany and Italy not merely was possible, but that it would be more profitable than friendship with Britain. These arguments were particularly appealing to the kind of Frenchman who had never really understood that an alliance has two sides—that a French alliance with Czecho-Slovakia, Poland or Great Britain, for example, meant not merely that Czechs, Poles or British would have to fight for France, but that the French might have to fight for them, even in unpropitious circumstances. The revelation from time to time that the category of Frenchmen who thought in this manner included certain important leaders weakened French prestige in nations allied to France and handicapped French foreign policy whenever it tried to follow a strong line.

Then there was the disintegrating effect of a long winter of waiting and inactivity, already mentioned earlier in these pages. The eight months from September 3 to May 10 certainly seem not to have been properly exploited. In May the fortifications along the Franco-Belgian frontier proved entirely inadequate. The nature of the terrain near the coast precluded deep fortifications like those of the Maginot Line; there is water everywhere a few feet below the surface. Yet it seems that attention might more usefully have been concentrated during the winter on strengthening that part of the line than on continuing to perfect the defensive casements of the Maginot Line proper. Nor must we fail to mention the censorship, often stupid and bureaucratic, which tried to keep the French people unaware of the dangers they faced, and succeeded down to the very end.

To some extent, too, French military errors can perhaps be traced to the fact that many older officers at the top were jealous of the younger men and automatically mistrusted the tactics which they favored. At least one eminent French chieftain disliked the whole idea of a mechanized army because, he said, mechanics are sure to be radicals. After the disastrous Battle of Charleroi on August 21, 1914, the French Army purged quantities of older officers who had proved themselves incompetent in the field. In those days there was more than one battle.

(5) *The German Army had superior resources, organization and striking power.*

The German economy under Hitler was a war economy. The Germany Army under Hitler always had the total material resources of Germany at its disposal, something inconceivable in a democratic country except in time of actual war.

The German Army seems also to have been directed by

more original and more aggressive minds than those in charge
of the French General Staff. This may have been merely the
natural psychological result of the fact that 1918 had been a
great victory for France, which tended to make French generals complacent about the superiority of their tactics, whereas
for Germany it had been a great defeat, which stung the
German generals into restudying all their old conceptions and
seeking new methods and instruments for regaining their
military power. Another reason may have been that Hitler
weeded out any older officer who dared oppose him when he
wanted to take risks or who criticized new conceptions of
strategy based on modern instruments of attack. Hitler also
understands the relationship between military and political
policy and has a nice sense of "timing." It may have been
luck that the May 10 attack was launched while the leaders
both of Britain and of France were preoccupied with a political
crisis. Or it may be that Hitler had been ready for some time
to attack at the first propitious moment and that the news he
received from London and Paris in the first week of May convinced him that the moment had arrived.

Novel tactics and new methods and instruments of war also
appealed to Hitler and his entourage enormously. They took
instantly to the idea of parachutists, first developed in Soviet
Russia. Air infantry, dive bombers used as artillery, tanks
used *en masse,* each of them connected by wireless with low-
flying planes, all became pets for which unlimited funds were
available. Meanwhile the German Foreign Office, the German
Army, the Gestapo and the *Auslands-Organisation* collabo-

rated in the careful preparation of an extensive service of resident fifth columnists in all potentially enemy countries. They
were to spy and to sabotage before war came; and after war
had come they were to be ready to coöperate with invading
parachutists, air infantry and advance motorcycle units in dis-
rupting communications and in spreading terror and confusion
among the civilian population back of the lines. Every detail
was planned in the most painstaking manner.

Not only was Germany superior to France in weight of metal,
weight of manpower, and numbers of planes; she was also
superior in initiative and organization.

Chapter XI

WHAT ARE THE LESSONS FOR US?

SIX YEARS AGO I tried to define the three courses which at that
time seemed to be open to France. They were, briefly: (1)
France might hold the German Government rigidly to its treaty
undertakings; seize gages, perhaps in the Rhineland, if German
rearmament continued; step up her own armaments, lengthen
the term of French military service, consolidate her alliances;
in a word, "sacrifice everything to the task of keeping 42
million Frenchmen one degree more powerful than 65 million
Germans." (2) France might give up her alliances in Eastern
Europe, washing her hands of responsibility for the spread of
German power in that direction, perhaps even going so far as
to conclude an alliance with Germany defining the future rôle
of each nation. That is to say, instead of fighting for the fruits
of the great victory of 1918 she could restrict her sphere of
interests and responsibilities, carrying on as the intellectual and
artistic center of Western Europe, developing the trade recom-
mended by her own special talents and resources, and leaving
the Nazi Government to do pretty much as it wished in the
greater world outside. (3) France might "adopt the second
procedure for a time, out of a mixture of indecision, internal
dissension, sincere pacifism and unwillingness to assume respon-

sibility for a fresh international crisis and possible bloodshed."
And then, "suddenly rousing her spirit," she might decide to
oppose a Germany which by that time had thoroughly rearmed
and possibly added to its own manpower the manpower of
Austria.

I suggested that the first course, though highly dangerous,
would not necessarily lead to general war; that the second
would not necessarily lead to general war either, though the
relentless extension of Nazi power would doubtless provoke
wars in Eastern Europe; but that the third definitely meant
war, "perhaps a long war," and "with the upshot in doubt." [1]

That was in 1934. Hitler had been in power in Germany
only a year. But already it was plain that the scroll History
was preparing to unroll was exceedingly black. She unrolled
it with amazing speed.

In March of the next year Nazi Germany formally de-
nounced the disarmament clauses in the Treaty of Versailles.
In September Mussolini attacked Ethiopia. In March 1936
Hitler sent his troops into the Rhineland. In May the Italian
armies reached Addis Ababa; sanctions had failed, the League
had failed. In July General Franco began his revolt against
the Spanish Republic. In October came the proclamation of
the Rome-Berlin Axis. In March 1938 Germany seized and
occupied Austria. The Czech crisis now began, and came to a
head in September at Munich. Chamberlain signed a special
treaty of friendship with Hitler. Bonnet signed one with Ribbentrop. In March 1939 the Czecho-Slovak state was anni-

[1] "Europe Between Wars?" New York: Macmillan, 1934, pp. 79-81.

hilated. The same month Germany annexed Memel. In April Italy invaded and conquered Albania. The day this occurred Franco Spain joined Germany and Italy in the anti-Comintern Pact. Britain and France, meanwhile, were pledging aid to Poland, Rumania and Greece in case of attack. On August 23 the world was startled by the signature of the German-Soviet Pact. The lines were now drawn. On September 1 Germany invaded Poland. Two days later Britain and France turned their promises to Poland into deeds. The Second World War had begun.

Even this skeletonized recapitulation of the on-rush of European events from 1935 to September 1939 reveals that, faced by repeated manifestations of Nazi and Fascist aggression, the statesmen of Britain and France were confused, incredulous, divided, slow. When in the spring of 1939 they at last brought themselves to pledge aid to three East European nations, it was very late. Given the current state of their own military strength and the extent of Nazi military preparations, their action now must be considered to have been as rash as their inaction previously had been. What in fact had happened was that France (like England) had followed the third of the three possible courses which I had outlined in 1934. This was the course which inevitably meant war, with the result in doubt.

From the time Hitler came to power in Germany the ruling statesmen of Britain and France were guilty of two principal failures. One was a failure of the imagination. They failed to grasp the remorseless nature of their antagonist. They failed to believe that he meant what he said, and meant it literally.

They failed to understand that he never could be bought off cheap, that there was only one argument which could possibly curb the threat of his ambition: superior physical force and a willingness, in the last resort, to use it. Lacking sufficient imagination themselves they could not reach the imaginations of their peoples. A Clemenceau would have known instinctively that the French patrimony was in danger and would have scourged the French people until they knew it too. There was no Clemenceau. It was not until May and June of this year that Frenchmen suddenly saw the weaknesses and deficiencies of their situation and realized that these must have existed for a long time.

The second failure was a failure of the will. Most French statesmen (like most of their colleagues across the Channel) were weak at the critical moments when they should have been decisive. Their effort was not to lead public opinion so much as to ingratiate themselves with it. The public wanted peace. They should have been told that they could have peace but only at a high price. But this also would have been unpopular, for the public not merely wanted peace but in addition wanted not to pay taxes for armament expenditures and wanted not to serve long terms in the army. Some statesmen in moments of frank self-examination must have seen the worst coming. They cheered themselves up by hoping it would not come. Others frankly manoeuvred for what they thought was their own personal advantage. Others in their hearts preferred authoritarian to parliamentary régimes. Let me cite just three instances.

In the autumn of 1935 M. Pierre Laval, a former Socialist, was Foreign Minister. On October 11 the representatives of 51 nations voted to impose sanctions on Italy following her attack on Ethiopia. Britain knew that if war resulted the British Fleet would have to bear the brunt. She asked France whether in that emergency the Fleet could rely on having the use of French Mediterranean ports. Probably M. Laval did not really want to see Mussolini stopped. In any case he refused a clear answer. The resulting catastrophe was double, one for Europe, one for France. Britain held back from imposing extreme sanctions; Mussolini won; the League was disgraced. For France, M. Laval's lack of perspicacity meant that she was left more exposed vis-à-vis Germany than ever. The next years might have been very different if instead of cold-shouldering Britain he had accepted her request, requiring in return, however, a firm British promise of help in case Hitler took advantage of trouble in the Mediterranean to make any move elsewhere which Frence felt menaced her vital interests.

In March 1936 France acquiesced in Hitler's *coup de force* in the Rhineland. M. Flandin was Foreign Minister at the time, in a rather weak Sarraut Cabinet. Faced with Hitler's violation of the Versailles Treaty and also his violation of his own endorsement of the Locarno Treaties, M. Flandin at first vacillated. The advice of General Maurin, Minister of War, of M. Piétri, Minister of Marine, and of M. Déat, Minister of Air, was defeatist. Two members of the Cabinet—Premier Sarraut himself and M. Mandel—were brave and far-sighted enough to propose that France force Hitler to reverse himself and that she require Britain to support her. The whole idea was antipathetic to the British people and to the personification of their current ideas, Mr. Stanley Baldwin. M. Flandin at that time was known generally as "London's man." He joined the defeatists. His weakness and his subservience to London went so far that when he crossed the Channel a few days later he not merely made no attempt to win Britain to a strong course against Germany; he failed even to secure as *quid pro quo* that Britain should formally guarantee aid to France in case the acceptance of Germany's aggression on this occasion led Hitler to new aggressions in the future. It was a fatal moment in the post-war history of France. As André Siegfried remarked a few months later in a private conversation: "On March 7, 1936, we lost the next war."

A third example. At 2:15 A.M. on September 21, 1938, on the instructions of MM. Daladier and Bonnet, the French Minister in Prague presented President Beneš of Czecho-Slovakia with what was virtually an ultimatum. He must agree to a certain Anglo-French plan for the settlement of the Sudeten question or be prepared to stand up to Hitler alone. He had no choice but to accept. The excuse France gave for treating her ally in this way was that Britain refused to promise support for France if France in turn supported Czecho-Slovakia and if war with Germany ensued. But even Mr. Chamberlain was disconcerted when he found that Hitler, sensing the weakness and timidity of the British and French Governments, promptly raised his ante. By September 26 London's disillusionment with appeasement had gone so far that the British Government gave the French Government a clear promise that if in spite of everything Germany did actually attack Czecho-Slovakia, then Britain (and Russia) would stand by France if she went to Czecho-Slovakia's help. What did Foreign Minister Bonnet do when he heard of this British offer? He brushed it aside. Two days later the Munich Conference was arranged. As I have written in another place:[1] "Never since the formation of the Entente Cordiale in 1904 had London been willing in time of peace to make such a promise. Historians will speculate as to the manner in which a Poincaré would have utilized that categorical pledge, even at this eleventh hour, to line up behind Britain, France and Russia so solid a coalition of powers from the Baltic to the Aegean as would have thrown Mussolini back into neutrality and called Hitler's bluff." But a Poincaré and a Viviani were not determining the foreign policy of France in September 1938.

To sum up. A powerful but individualistic, pacifically inclined and divided people did not succeed in finding a way to let their imagination properly inform their temper. They were in mortal danger and did not know it. When French publicists told them they did not believe it. Their responsible statesmen were not among those who told them. The excuse that these put forward is that even if they had themselves grasped the truth and told it they would not have been believed either. But peace-loving as the French people were, and unpalatable as the truth about Germany would have been, the attempt to rouse them should have been made. It was not made, except

[1] "When There Is No Peace." New York: Macmillan, 1939, p. 98.

by M. Paul Reynaud; and when he was given the right to turn his warnings into acts it was, we now see, too late. To the failure of the French imagination was added a failure of the French will.

Today Nazi Germany instructs the United States of America to make a choice. We can choose our own heritage of freedom, won for us by our fathers and our grandfathers, and thus far preserved by ourselves. We can decide to maintain that freedom at any and all cost in a world which we hope may some day once again be free. Or we can accept the limited rôle which Chancellor Hitler and his partners in blackmail choose to assign us in *their* world. We can accept *their* ideas, *their* morals, *their* economy, *their* culture, *their* religion, *their* conception of the whole nature and duty of man.

Let us be thankful to France, for France had the same choice put to her in the years after 1933, and the lesson of what happened to her is before our eyes. She hesitated to make a firm choice. That hesitation was in itself a choice. In the end she rebelled against becoming the slave of a foreign and antipathetic ideology and a partner in Nazi crime. Her revulsion of feeling came too late, and her response to it was inadequate. She was not able to turn the oncoming Nazi tide. She has become a slave to the Nazis and, to an extent, their reluctant partner.

Let us, unlike France, have the power of imagination to discern the possible destinies that await us. Let us, unlike France, have the power of will to embrace the destiny that we choose, bravely, confidently, and in time.

INDEX OF PERSONS

unanimous vote of confidence, 22;
May 19 broadcast voicing confidence, 38; May 22 conference
with Weygand and Reynaud in
Paris, 45; May 23 address to
Commons, 47; May 26 conference with Reynaud, 54; address
on Belgian surrender, 58; June 4
address on Dunkerque, 65; recognizes émigré Belgian Government,
73; wires Reynaud promise of
more help, 77; consults Reynaud
at Tours, 84, 86; second visit to
Tours, 91; his views on armistice,
92; his requirements regarding
French fleet, 106; broadcasts Britain will fight alone, 110; June
18 address, "Battle of Britain is
about to begin," 115; appeal to
French people, 150; denounces
French armistice, 165; broadcasts
hope of French liberation, 168
Ciano, Count Galeazzo, transmits
Roosevelt's appeal to Mussolini,
29; Milan speech, 38; informs
French and British Ambassadors
of declaration of war, 77; at armistice talks, 153
Cooper, Alfred Duff, fruitless trip to
Rabat, 133
Corap, General André Georges,
commands French Ninth Army,
19; dismissed, 27; faulty tactics,
42; reported absent when attack
began, 44; his forces on Meuse
broken, 177
Cripps, Sir Stafford, heads trade
mission to Moscow, 57; Ambassador, 68, 89

Daladier, Edouard, conflict with
Reynaud, 6, 12; visits Leopold,
22; Foreign Minister, 35;
dropped from Cabinet, 71; boards

Massilia, 121; sails, 133; promises
defensive war, 175
Darlan, Admiral Jean, favors con-
tinued war, 105; Minister of
Navy and Merchant Marine, 106
Déat, Marcel, defeatist advice, 192
Delbos, Yvon, Minister of Educa-
tion, 71; favors continued war,
105; boards *Massilia,* 121
Dill, Lieutenant General Sir John
Greer, Chief of British Imperial
Staff, 54

Eden, Anthony, Secretary for War,
16; broadcasts after Dunkerque,
63

Flandin, Pierre-Étienne, and appeasement, 179, 192

Gamelin, General Maurice Gustave,
source of Reynaud-Daladier conflict, 6, 12; unsure of post, 7; Order of the Day of May 10, 11;
fears Germans may reach Paris
May 16, 31; May 17 Order of the
Day, 34; supplanted by Weygand, 38; British criticize him,
49; wanted show-down over
Rhineland coup, 174; plan of
campaign in Low Countries, 176
Gaulle, General Charles de, Under
Secretary in Defense Ministry,
71; acts as intermediary between
Churchill and Reynaud, 103; in
Bordeaux, 107; appeals to French
people to resist, 117, 148; cen-
sured by French Government,
123; cashiered, 152; announces
Provisional French National
Committee, 154; recognized by
Britain, 157; says fleet and Em-
pire will continue fight, 158
Gayda, Virginio, boasts Italian